THE
100+
SERIES™

Reproducible Activities

Words on the Vine

Grades 5-8

by
Claudia Vurnakes

Instructional Fair
An imprint of Carson-Dellosa Publishing LLC
Greensboro, North Carolina

Instructional Fair

Author: Claudia Vurnakes
Cover Artist: Elizabeth Adams
Interior Artist: Janet Skiles, Marty Bucella

Instructional Fair
An imprint of Carson-Dellosa Publishing LLC
PO Box 35665
Greensboro, NC 27425 USA

ISBN 978-1-56822-661-3
01-335118091

Table of Contents

Introduction

Who says ancient Latin and Greek are dead languages? They live on in the words we speak every day! And what valuable clues those ancient languages give us when we encounter bits of them in an unfamiliar word. Introduce students to the fun and challenge of word genealogy with this 36-unit vocabulary program based on common Latin and Greek roots. As a framework for your year-long word study, units may be presented weekly or in larger clusters throughout the year.

Each three-page reproducible unit introduces ten vocabulary words and traces their definitions back to a common meaning. On the upper corner of every page is a small visual clue, a memory-jogging picture that symbolizes the root. Your students examine the words in context to understand correct usage; then they put them to work in creative and challenging assignments. To enliven your program even more, pull in activities from the enrichment ideas given with the master word lists at the front of this book.

With easy-to-remember visual clues, passages that are fun to read, and hands-on activities, *Words on the Vine* seeks to reach learners of every style. Instilling a fascination for words is a life-enhancing gift you can give your students; we hope this book helps make that goal a reality.

Master Word Lists and Enrichment Activities

FOLI—leaf
Unit words: bifoliate, defoliant, exfoliate, foliage, folic acid, folio, portfolio, trefoil, foil, unifoliate
Additional words: quatrefoil, cinquefoil, octofoil, foliation
Enrichment activities:
*Instruct students to make designs of their choice of leaf pattern. Fill the shapes with FOLI words.
*Assign current events research on the defoliant used in Vietnam, Agent Orange.
*Which popular brand of vitamin supplements contains folic acid? Send your class shoppers to the drug store to do some scouting.

MISS/MITT—to send
Unit words: commissioner, smite, transmit, submissive, missive, remittance, missile, missionary, permit, admissible
Additional words: manumit, emit, transmission, omit, emissary, promise, surmise, demise
Enrichment activities:
*Give mechanically-minded students the task of explaining the function of a car's transmission. Then use students to pantomime the various parts working together: engine, axle, gear, shaft.
*What role did missionaries play in the settlement of America? Was it positive, negative, or a mixture of both?

MANU—hand
Unit words: manufacture, manual, manuscript, manicure, manacle, manager, manipulate, maneuver, mandate, emancipate
Additional words: manumission, maniple, manifest
Enrichment activities:
*Display examples of illuminated manuscripts. Provide materials for students to create similar drawings of their own initials.
*Have students research the methods slave-traders of the 1800s used to capture and manacle African tribesmen.
*From what do your students wish to be emancipated? Their lists will be revealing—and surprising.

MAL—bad
Unit words: malevolent, malapropism, malicious, malodorous, malady, malaria, malediction, malefactor, malignant, malpractice
Additional words: malversation, maladroit, malaise, malfeasance, malnutrition
Enrichment activities:
*Send students to the library to discover how malaria spreads. How did wrong ideas influence the name of this disease?
*Who is Mrs. Malaprop?
*Archie Bunker, from the 70s TV show *All in the Family*, was infamous for his malapropisms. Challenge rerun-watchers to make a collection of his misused words.

GEN—birth, origin
Unit words: progeny, generous, genius, gender, genteel, generic, generation, genesis, genuine, indigenous
Additional words: disingenuous, genetic, generatrix, oxygen, general, generalization, genocide, gentry, gentleman
Enrichment activities:
*Locate copies of Mensa intelligence tests. Encourage students to assess their brain-power.
*For a writing assignment, challenge students to write opinion papers plagued with sweeping generalizations, then rewrite them using specific statements.
*Are generic foods as tasty as brand names? Conduct your own classroom taste tests.

GEO/TERR—earth
Unit words: geology, geometry, terrace, subterranean, geode, inter, geography, Mediterranean, geocentric, terrain
Additional words: extra-terrestrial, geomancy, geophagy, geoponics, territory, terrier, terrarium, terra cotta
Enrichment activities:
*Display geodes in class. Discuss their formation.
*Prepare a time capsule to inter on the school grounds.
*Two-liter plastic drink bottles make great terrariums. After planting and watering, tighten the caps to keep moisture in.
*Dog-lovers will enjoy digging up the background on the terrier breed.

PED/POD—foot
Unit words: podiatrist, pedestal, pedestrian, centipede, quadruped, pedal, pedometer, impediment, tripod, pedicure
Additional words: orthopedic, pedigree, pediment, velocipede, amphipod, podium, arthropod
Enrichment activities:
*Challenge students to find out how many legs a centipede actually has (42).
*What buildings in your town have pediments?
*Borrow a pedometer students can use to clock the distances they walk in a typical school day.

ASTR/STELL—star
Unit words: astronomy, astrologer, asteroid, aster, stellar, constellation, stelliform, asterisk, disaster, astrodome
Additional words: astral, Astraea, astrolabe, astronomical, interstellar
Enrichment activities:
*Go star-gazing! Point out well-known constellations.
*Pot some asters to brighten up the classroom.
*How many songs can students list that mention stars? Divide into teams for a little competition.
*Assign independent research on the origins of the zodiac.

CHRON/TEMP—time
Unit words: anachronism, chronicles, chronic, chronometer, temporary, extemporaneous, contemporary, tempo, synchronize, tempest
Additional words: tempestuous, temporal, tempus fugit, contretemps

Enrichment activities:
*Keep a supply of interesting questions handy for extemporaneous speaking.
*Challenge students to write short stories full of humorous anachronisms.
*Construct a potato-powered chronometer. Kits and directions are available at most science stores.

AQUA/HYDRA—water
Unit words: aquamarine, aquatic, hydrophobia, aquarelle, hydraulic, aqueduct, hydroponic, hydrant, Aquarius, aqueous
Additional words: aquarium, aquacade, aquaplane, aquaculture, hydrogen, aquarist, aqualung, hydropathy, hydrothermal, hydrozoan
Enrichment activities:
*Root potato eyes for some classroom aquaculture.
*Assign research on the aquamarine gemstone. For what medicinal purposes did the ancient Romans use it? (To cure laziness and build courage.)
*Provide plastic tubing, straws, and duct tape for hands-on aqueduct construction.

MOB/MOT—move
Unit words: commotion, remote, demote, nonmotile, promote, immobile, locomotion, unmotivated, emotion, automobile
Additional words: emote, motive, motor, mobile
Enrichment activities:
*Students will enjoy pantomiming unit words for classmates to guess.
*To what remote part of the world would your students like to travel? Why?
*Stage a classroom commotion and then ask students to report exactly what happened. Discuss how distraction alters our perceptions.

CAP—head
Unit words: capitulate, caparison, decapitate, recapitulate, cape, capitalism, cap, capricious, capital, captain
Additional words: capitol, capuchin monkey
Enrichment activities:
*Provide fabric scraps, needles, and thread for some crazy cap and cape construction. What super heroes do students become when they don their creations?
*Horse-lovers will enjoy researching dressage, the competitions in which riders guide their caparisoned horses through specific movements.

MATER/PATER—mother, father
Unit words: patrician, patron, pattern, patriarch, patronym, maternity, alma mater, matrix, matrimony, matricide
Additional words: matron, patrimony, patricide, matriarch, paternity, patriot, matriculant, matronymic, patronize, matriculate
Enrichment activities:
*Challenge students to write songs honoring their alma mater. Use well-known tunes so everyone can sing along.
*Who said,"Ask not what your country can do for you—ask what you can do for your country?" (John F. Kennedy). Discuss patriotism with your students. Is it an outmoded value?

BENE/BON—good
Unit words: bounteous, bona fide, benediction, bonanza, bonus, benevolent, bon vivant, beneficiary, benign, benefactor
Additional words: pro bono, bonny, bonbon, bon mot, bon voyage, benison
Enrichment activities:
*With a hot plate or portable microwave, cook up some saucepan bonbons. (Check cookbooks for simple recipes.) Don't forget to say a benediction before munching!
*Throw a bon voyage party complete with confetti and streamers. What gifts would be suitable to give a world-traveler?

JECT/JET—throw
Unit words: injection, jettison, interjection, subject, reject, dejection, eject, projectile, trajectory, projection
Additional words: subjective, jetsam, jet, jetty, abject, objective
Enrichment activities:
*Challenge students to create their own comic books complete with G-rated interjections.
*The discoveries of the rabies and smallpox injections fascinate students. Locate biographies of Edward Jenner and Louis Pasteur for supplemental reading.

FLAM/PYRO—fire
Unit words: flammable, pyre, flamboyant, pyrotechnics, inflammatory, pyromania, inflammation, pyrite, pyrophobia, pyrography
Additional words: flambeau, Pyrex, pyrope, pyrostat, pyrotoxin, pyroxene
Enrichment Activities:
*Send students to fashion magazines to cut out examples of flamboyant dress.
*Assign independent research on the legend of the phoenix, born anew in the flames of a funeral pyre.

PRIM/PRIN/PROTO—first
Unit words: principle, prima donna, protocol, primer, primeval, prince, primogenitor, principality, protagonist, primary
Additional words: primal, prim, primrose, primordial, primipara, princess, principal, protomartyr, protoplasm, protozoan
Enrichment activities:
*Prepare a list of students' favorite fiction. Challenge the class to identify as many protagonists as possible.
*Send home a family project—to boil down the five basic principles that parents and children hope to live by.
*Read Longfellow's poem *The Song of Hiawatha* to the class: "This is the forest primeval. . ."

ROTA/VOLV—turn
Unit words: revolution, evolution, voluminous, volume, vault, rotate, voluble, rotund, rotunda, rotisserie
Additional words: rotagraph, rotor, rotifer, devolve, involvement
Enrichment activities:
*Stage a debate on evolution versus creationism. Does the fossil evidence support our teaching of the last 50 years?
*Construct a hand-turned rotisserie that uses solar power to cook hot dogs.
*Assign sketches showing construction of the vaulted ceiling and the rotunda.

COR—heart

Unit words: accord, discord, concord, concordance, courage, cordial, encourage, discourage, record, accordion

Additional words: cordate

Enrichment activities:

*Display several concordances and provide practice in using them.

*Invite an accordion player to demonstrate his instrument.

*Discuss the difference between encouragement and discouraging remarks. Role-play friendship situations to dramatize the two words.

*Play a recording of "mystery sounds." Challenge students to identify them.

RECT/REG—king

Unit words: regal, rectitude, rectangle, regalia, regicide, regime, regimen, rector, erect, regulation

Additional words: reign, correct, viceroy, region, regent, address, director, royalty, dress, resurrect, regiment

Enrichment activities:

*Give students the task of designing regalia for odd situations. They may sketch or assemble their ideas.

*What regimens do successful people follow? Challenge students to interview or correspond with positive role models.

*What local issues are begging for regulation? Hold classroom debates on what types of rules are needed and why.

MONO/UNI—one

Unit words: monastery, monotone, monophobia, union, unison, monogamy, unique, monopoly, monocle, monolith

Additional words: uniform, monarch, monosyllabic, universe, monomania, monogram, unicorn, monotheism, monologue, monochromatic

Enrichment activities:

*Play recordings of monastic chants.

*Ask the class to come up with theories—why and how did the ancient Druids erect the monoliths at Stonehenge?

*Create your own Monopoly game, customized to your school and town.

BI/DU—two

Unit words: bicuspid, biped, bicep, bicentennial, bifocal, bilingual, dialogue, duet, duel, duplicity

Additional words: bicycle, bigamy, bisect, binocular, dual, duplicate, duplex, billion, bihourly, bifurcate, bifacial, biracial

Enrichment activities:

*Research and stage a mock duel in class.

*When was/is your state's bicentennial? Plan ways to celebrate.

*Which Roman god was bifacial? Why?

TRI/QUAD/QUINT/PENT/DEC/CENT

Unit words: trident, trilogy, quadruped, quadragenarian, pentagon, quintuplet, Decalogue, decapod, century, centipede

Additional words: triplicate, centenarian, pentagram, decasyllabic, centigrade, trisect, quartet, quintessence, December, quadrilateral, decimate, trinity, centurion, decagon, Pentateuch

Enrichment activities:
*Challenge students to correctly draw and label geometric shapes that correspond to the number roots.
*Ask duos, trios, quartets to sing for the class.

SPEC/SPIC—look
Unit words: spectacle, spectator, conspicuous, specter, spectrum, suspicious, speculate, specimen, retrospective, speculum
Additional words: inspector, circumspect, species, suspect, expectation, respect
Enrichment activities:
*Have available prisms for examining the spectrum. Challenge students to memorize the colors in order.
*Assign a retrospective writing assignment in which students take a fond look back at some key moment in their lives.
*Invite a stock broker to explain how investors speculate, the pros and cons.
*What are the key elements of respect—how does one extend it, how does one earn it?

GRAPH/GRAM—write
Unit words: autobiography, autograph, biography, cardiogram, epigraph, grammar, graphics, graphology, orthography, paragraph
Additional words: bibliography, geography, monogram, hologram, pentagram, telegram, photography
Enrichment activities:
*Locate graphology handbooks for students to use to analyze one another's handwriting.
*Schedule a biography-reading blitz.
*Invite a cardiologist to "read" a cardiogram to students.

CARN/CORP—flesh, body
Unit words: carnival, carnage, carnivore, reincarnation, corpse, esprit de corps, corpuscle, corporation, corpulence, corsage
Additional words: carnation, incorporate, corporal, corset, corporeal
Enrichment activities:
*Stage a classroom carnival.
*Plan and design a menu that carnivores will crave.
*Assign research on the reincarnation beliefs of Hinduism.
*Challenge students to develop a business plan for their own school-based corporation.

CURR/CURS/COURS—run
Unit words: current, curriculum, courier, cursive, precursor, corsair, courser, cursory, discourse, corridor
Additional words: occur, recur, recourse, currency, corral,
Enrichment activities:
*What courses would students take if they could design their own curriculum?
*The histories of real pirates make for fascinating and sad reading. The swash-buckling life is not all it's cracked up to be! Check out Blackbeard, Stede Bonnet, Sir Francis Drake, Captain Greaves, William Kidd, Jean Laffite, Sir Henry Morgan, Anne Bonny.

ARCH—ruler
Unit words: archenemy, monarch, archangel, anarchy, archive, archrival, architect, hierarchy, archetype, archipelago

Additional words: matriarch, patriarch, oligarchy, archbishop, archduke (plus close cousins from the archae root: archaic, archaeopteryx, archaeology)
Enrichment activities:
*Plan an imaginary trip to an archipelago complete with travel brochures, packing lists, and itineraries.
*Display photos of buildings designed by famous architects.

CYCL/ORB—roundness
Unit words: tricycle, cyclone, cycle, cyclops, encyclopedia, cyclostome, orb, exorbitant, orbit, periorbital
Additional words: suborbital, orbicular, bicycle, unicycle, recycle, cylinder, cyclorama
Enrichment activities:
*What causes cyclones? View a portion of the movie *Twister*.
*Stage a scavenger hunt to expose students to the wide variety of encyclopedias available.
*Borrow a unicycle and encourage students to ride.
*Diagram the orbits of the different planets on your classroom ceiling.

MIN—small
Unit words: mince, miniature, minimum, minuet, minuscule, minute, minister, minus, minor, minstrel
Additional words: minority, minify, minim, minuend, minimalist, minion, diminish, administration, minutia
Enrichment activities:
*Prepare a dish containing miniature marshmallows.
*Assign independent research on medieval minstrels.
*Play recordings of minuets—learn to dance to them!
*Take a school census. What minority groups does your school population include?

PHON—sound
Unit words: euphony, cacophony, symphony, phonics, microphone, homophone, xylophone, phonolite, antiphony, aphonia
Additional words: telephone, phonograph, phonology, phoneme, megaphone, phonate, phonometer
Enrichment activities:
*Listen to well-known symphonies
*Review basic phonics skills with students.
*Challenge the class to write and perform original antiphonal songs.
*Compile a master list of common homophones. Post it on the wall to add to throughout the year.

ANTHRO/HOMO/HUM—man
Unit words: misanthrope, anthropology, anthropocentric, anthropomorphize, *Homo sapiens*, homicide, homage, humane, anthropophagous, humanitarian
Additional words: philanthropist, hombre, humanism, anthropography, anthropoid, anthropometry, hominoid, humanity
Enrichment activities:
*Display and discuss drawings of developmental man.
*Create anthropomorphic puppets from common household items.
*Assign research on flesh-eating bacteria.
*Challenge students to write letters of homage to their parents.

DICT—speak
Unit words: diction, dictionary, edict, predict, contradict, verdict, dictation, dictator, dictum, indictment
Additional words: benediction, malediction, Dictaphone
Enrichment activities:
*Explore the multi-volumed *Oxford English Dictionary*.
*Invite a judge or lawyer to speak about the jury process and rendering verdicts.
*Watch portions of the classic movie *My Fair Lady*, in which Eliza Doolittle learns proper diction.

PORT—carry
Unit words: portal, export, deportation, deportment, portable, portage, portcullis, porter, support, transport
Additional words: port, import, comportment, portfolio, reporter, important, portmanteau, portly, portamento, portiere
Enrichment activities:
*Visit a shipping terminal or customs office.
*Research the laws governing U.S. imports and exports.
*Write rules of deportment for twenty-first-century students.
*Challenge students to map out castle designs, from moat and portcullis to dungeon.

SYM/SYN—together, same
Unit words: sympathy, symmetry, synagogue, symptom, syndicate, synthetic, synonym, symbiosis, symposium, photosynthesis
Additional words: symphony, symbol, synchronize, syncretism, syndactyl, synergism, syntax
Enrichment activities:
*Make symmetrical inkblot designs. What do students see in them?
*Students will enjoy reading about Charles Goodyear's efforts to develop synthetic rubber.
*Send the class looking for symbiotic pairs: mistletoe and the host tree, crocodiles and the birds that clean their teeth, cyclostomes and the large host fish.

PHIL—love
Unit words: philanthropist, philosophy, bibliophile, philharmonic, philoprogenitive, philatelist, philander, philodendron, philter, necrophile
Additional words: philology, Philadelphia, philogyny, philhellenic, Francophile
Enrichment activities:
*Invite a philatelist to display his/her collection.
*Grow a philodendron in class.
*Assign independent research on philters down through the ages.

Leaf Lovers

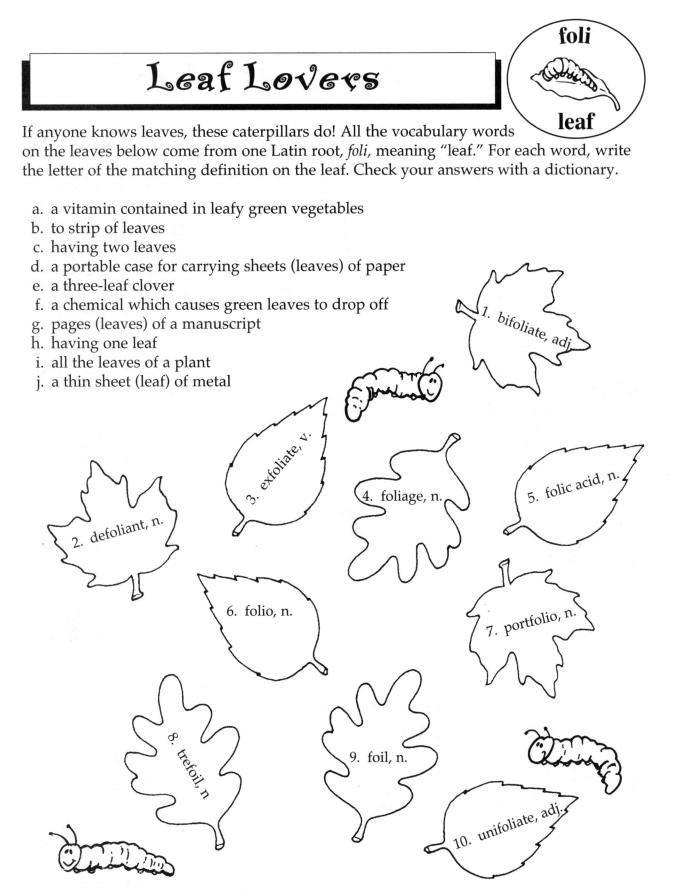

foli

leaf

If anyone knows leaves, these caterpillars do! All the vocabulary words on the leaves below come from one Latin root, *foli*, meaning "leaf." For each word, write the letter of the matching definition on the leaf. Check your answers with a dictionary.

a. a vitamin contained in leafy green vegetables
b. to strip of leaves
c. having two leaves
d. a portable case for carrying sheets (leaves) of paper
e. a three-leaf clover
f. a chemical which causes green leaves to drop off
g. pages (leaves) of a manuscript
h. having one leaf
i. all the leaves of a plant
j. a thin sheet (leaf) of metal

1. bifoliate, adj.
2. defoliant, n.
3. exfoliate, v.
4. foliage, n.
5. folic acid, n.
6. folio, n.
7. portfolio, n.
8. trefoil, n
9. foil, n.
10. unifoliate, adj.

Now cut out each leaf. On the back side, write a sentence using the vocabulary word. With string, tape, and a twig, you can make a *foli* mobile.

foli

leaf

Comic Re-Leaf

Match each cartoon with the correct vocabulary word. Write the words on the lines.

1. _____

2. _____

3. _____

bifoliate
defoliant
exfoliate
foil
foliage
folic acid
folio
portfolio
trefoil
unifoliate

4. _____

5. _____

6. _____

7. _____

8. _____

9. _____

10. _____

How lucky can you get? Turn your paper over and draw these lucky clovers: a quatrefoil, a cinquefoil, and an octofoil. Next, write the definitions for your ten vocabulary words. Make certain you include the root meaning *leaf* for each word.

Turn Over a New Leaf

foli

leaf

Here are some wacky newspaper headlines. For each one, write the first sentence of the story, defining the vocabulary words. The first one has been done for you.

1. Unicorn Uncovers Unusual Unifoliate Under Uncle's Umbrella: Yesterday, a young unicorn playing in the park moved the umbrella of a family member only to find a rare species of plant having only one leaf.

2. Folic Acid Found to Foster Fancy Footwork in Frozen Finns: _____
   _____
   _____

3. Experts Experienced in Exfoliation Expect Extra Exercise This Spring: _____
   _____
   _____

4. Troubling Trail of Tricolor Trefoils Traced to Trio of Trolls: _____
   _____
   _____

5. Beautiful Bifoliate Bellflower Bursts into Bloom, Baffling Biologists: _____
   _____
   _____

6. Found: Folio and Fountain Pen Felt to Be Frankenstein's Father's:_____
   _____
   _____

7. Who Took the Kids' Candy? Police Point to Painter Pushing Peppermint-Packed Portfolio Across Public Pumpkin Patch:_____
   _____
   _____

8. Defoliant's Foes Defend Endangered Fig in Deforestation Fight: _____
   _____
   _____

9. Fragile Foil Football Flies Fifty Feet; Fractures Figures in Famous Fact Book: _____
   _____
   _____

10. Freeze Frosts Fall Foliage; Forget Festival Frenzy, Faculty Says
    _____
    _____

Now, choose a headline and illustrate it. See whether a friend can match your drawing to the correct headline.

miss, mitt
to send

Mission to Mars

The Latin roots *miss, mitt* mean "to send." All the vocabulary words below can really send you places! Write the letter of the matching definition for each word on its missile. Check your answers with a dictionary.

a. a rocket or weapon sent through the air
b. a person sent for a special task, usually religious
c. a message sent through the mail
d. to send from one person or place to another
e. yielding; obedient
f. a person sent to meet with others to plan and make official decisions
g. money sent in payment
h. to send a sharp blow; to strike
i. to allow; to authorize
j. able to be sent as truthful evidence

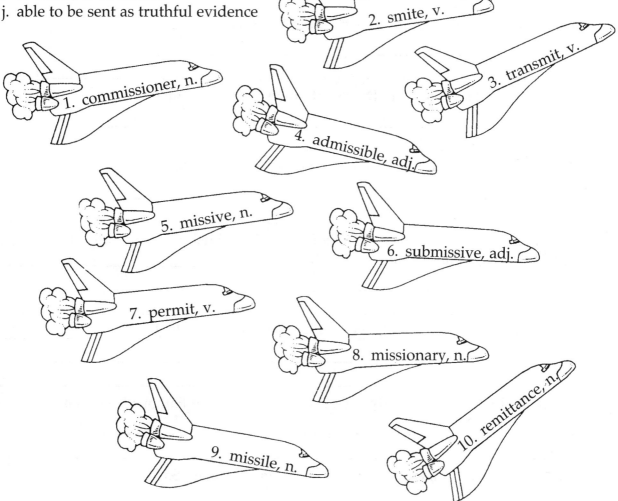

1. commissioner, n.
2. smite, v.
3. transmit, v.
4. admissible, adj.
5. missive, n.
6. submissive, adj.
7. permit, v.
8. missionary, n.
9. missile, n.
10. remittance, n.

Blast off! On the back of this sheet, use the vocabulary word in an original sentence of seven words or more.

Interplanetary P. O.

miss, mitt to send

A shuttle collision has scattered mail all over the galaxy. Read each letter and fill in the missing vocabulary word.

1. Dear Mr. and Mrs. Zixx, Will you _____ me to call on your daughter Yinny when I visit Pluto two eons from now?

2. Sir: We are a peaceful race. We will allow no armed _____ or other weapons of war on the planet Xeres.

3. To: Families of Martian Wilderness Campers. Send all _____ and care packages of goodies to the camp address below.

4. Dearest Borgo, Cupid's arrows _____ my heart. I can't wait for your next visit! Can't you come next eon?

5. People of Xeres: We come in peace, to share with you news of our God. We are _____, not men of war.

6. To: Comet Comics. Please send me two copies of *Galaxy Girl*. Enclosed is my _____ of $33,675.95.

7. Dear Wronz, As your lawyer, I must advise you that gossip is not _____ evidence in Mercury's courts.

8. Dear Yinny, I hope you plan to be an obedient and _____ wife.

9. To: Communications Specialist, Saturn. From: ComSpec, Venus. Your satellite signal will not _____. Have you vacuumed your lunar dust lately?

10. To: Pluto Marriage and Family _____.
From: Yinny Zixx. Please advise me on the board's decision concerning the following question. Do twenty-fifth century Plutonian spouses obey each other?

Now turn your paper over and write a synonym for each of these vocabulary words.

miss, mitt
to send

What on Earth?

Read the clues below and match them to the correct rhyming pair. There may be nothing new under the sun, but it shines on some strange things!

What do you call

_____ 1. an unshaven person traveling for religious purposes?

_____ 2. a missive written on a pullover?

_____ 3. a young cat struck by love?

_____ 4. remittance for bees' work?

_____ 5. a fog permitted to form?

_____ 6. a collapsible canvas dwelling transmitted from L. L. Bean?

_____ 7. a miniature missile?

_____ 8. submissive wildlife?

_____ 9. the commissioner of good books?

_____ 10. admissible dental records?

a. honey money
b. a pocket rocket
c. tooth truth
d. a letter sweater
e. a smitten kitten
f. tame game
g. a hairy missionary
h. an allowed cloud
i. a sent tent
j. the reader leader

Do you ever wonder why? Here is your chance to go as far out of this world as you want. Read each situation below and answer the question.

A. An elderly citizen smites a county commissioner with her pocketbook.
Why?_____

_____

B. The sheriff's department fails to transmit admissible evidence to court.
Why?_____

_____

C. The inhabitants of a planet will not permit a strange missile to land.
Why?_____

_____

D. None of the missives written by a missionary make it home. Why?_____

_____

E. For once, a millionaire is submissively sending the government its remittance on April 15th. Why?_____

_____

Hand In Hand

manu hand

Knowing your vocabulary roots certainly comes in handy! When you learn that the Latin root *manu* means "hand," you have a clue to every word listed below. Write the letter of the definition on the right in the matching mitten on the left. Use a dictionary to check your answers.

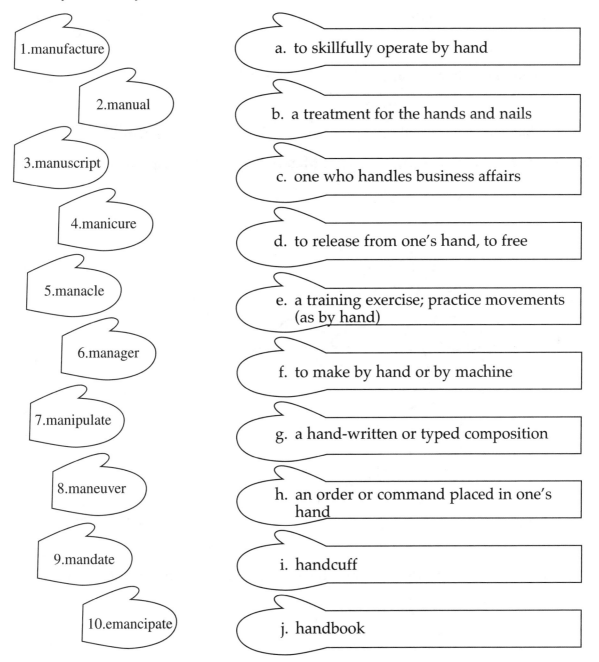

1. manufacture

2. manual

3. manuscript

4. manicure

5. manacle

6. manager

7. manipulate

8. maneuver

9. mandate

10. emancipate

a. to skillfully operate by hand

b. a treatment for the hands and nails

c. one who handles business affairs

d. to release from one's hand, to free

e. a training exercise; practice movements (as by hand)

f. to make by hand or by machine

g. a hand-written or typed composition

h. an order or command placed in one's hand

i. handcuff

j. handbook

Cut out all the mittens. Connect the matching pairs with lengths of yarn or ribbon to make vocabulary bookmarks. Place them in your books so you can review your vocabulary every time you sit down to read this week.

manu
hand

Hand Done

Experts say you can learn much by studying a person's hand. Meet Mandy. Draw the details listed below on Mandy's hand.

1. Give Mandy a manicure.

2. Place a manacle on Mandy.

3. Manufacture a ring and glue it on Mandy's finger.

4. Emancipate the butterfly trapped in Mandy's hand.

5. Draw an ant maneuvering around Mandy's thumb.

6. Show what excessive pencil manipulation has done to Mandy's hand.

7. Show the manual manuscript Manager Mandy has been writing. Include a suitable title.

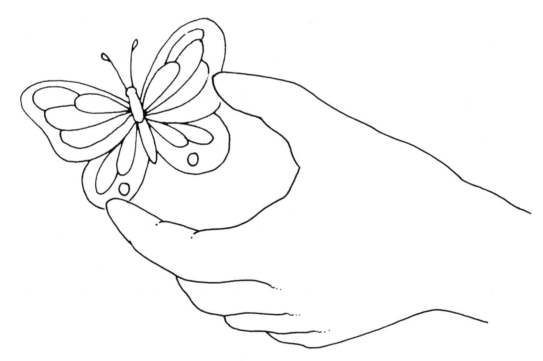

Study Mandy's hand. What do you think she is like? Write your description of Mandy on the back of your paper.

All Hands on Deck

manu
hand

To do his job right, a pirate needs a swift ship and a trustworthy treasure map. For each item listed below, look in the answer bank to find the person who needs that item the most. Write the correct match in the space provided and explain your choice.

Who needs . . .   Why?

1. a manicure? _____ _____

2. a manacle? _____ _____

3. a mandate from the people? _____ _____

4. a manuscript? _____ _____

5. a manual? _____ _____

6. a manufacturer? _____ _____

7. a strict manager? _____ _____

8. a training maneuver? _____ _____

9. emancipation? _____ _____

10. a manipulator? _____ _____

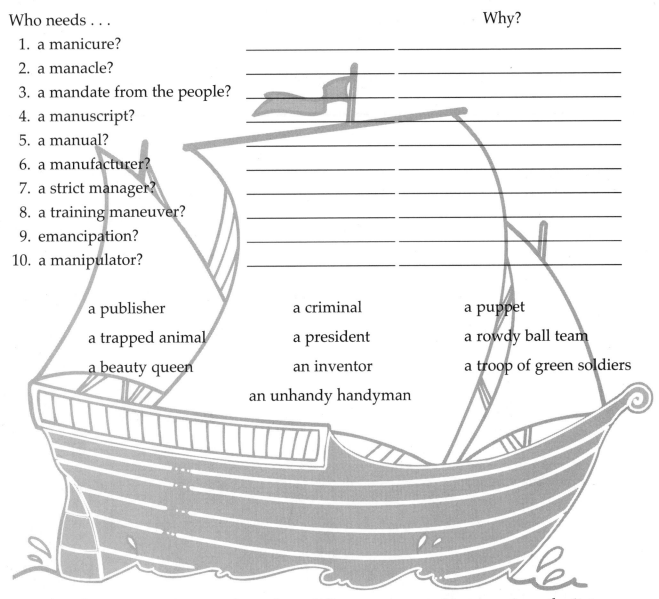

a publisher	a criminal	a puppet
a trapped animal	a president	a rowdy ball team
a beauty queen	an inventor	a troop of green soldiers
	an unhandy handyman	

Now stir things up! Make up at least three different crazy combinations from the lists above. See if a friend can create some equally crazy reasons why!

Example: Why would a criminal need a manicure? If he were appearing on the hot new TV show, *Stars Behind Bars*.

mal

bad

Write and Wrong

Here are some of the bad guys from the world of words. They all share the Latin root *mal*, meaning "bad" or "wrong." For each word listed below, write the letter of the correct definition. Next, circle the correct pronunciation. Use a dictionary to check your answers.

a. desiring harm to someone or something else
b. bad or harmful, producing death
c. illness believed to be spread by bad air, actually spread by mosquitoes
d. performing one's duty in a bad or wrong way
e. bad-smelling
f. one who does wrong; a villain
g. having bad feelings toward someone or something; spite, hatred
h. bad speech; a curse
i. a bad health condition; a disease
j. a word used the wrong way; usually with humorous results

		Column 1	Column 2	Column 3
_____	1. malevolent	mă - lĕv´- ō - lĕnt	mā - lĕ - vō´- lĕnt	māl- ĕ - vō´- lĕnt
_____	2. malapropism	măl - ă - prŏp´- ĭsm	mă - lă´- prŏp - ĭsm	măl´- ă - prŏp - ĭsm
_____	3. malicious	măl - ĭ - cē´- ŭs	mă -lĭsh´- ŭs	măl- i´- shŭs
_____	4. malodorous	măl - ō´- der - ŭs	mal - ŏ - door´- us	măl - ō - der - ŭs´
_____	5. malady	mă - lā´- dē	măl´- ă - dĭ	măl - ă - dĭ´
_____	6. malaria	mă - lar - ī´- a	mā - lar - ēe´- a	mă - lăr´- ĭ - a
_____	7. malediction	măl - ĕ - dĭk´- shun	māl - dĭk - tĭ´- un	māl´- dĭk - zhun
_____	8. malefactor	māl - făk´- tor	măl´- ĕ - făk - ter	māl - făk´- ter
_____	9. malignant	māl´- lĭn - ant	mă - lĭ - nănt´	mă - lĭg´- nănt
_____	10. malpractice	măl - prăk´- tĭs	māl´- prăk - tĭc	măl - prăk - tĭs´

Rest In Peace

mal

bad

Not knowing words can be deadly! For each tombstone clue below, write the most suitable vocabulary word.

1. Here lies the body
   of Mildred Pink,
   Done in by the stink
   From her kitchen sink.
   _____

2. When I got sick,
   says Pauline Peters,
   Was it bad air—
   Or was it 'skeeters?
   _____

3. Blarney Barney
   Using the wrong word
   was my curse.
   Oh well, things could
   have been verse.
   _____

4. Here lies the body of
   Muscles McMillian,
   known by all as
   our town villain.
   _____

5. Roosevelt Ruth
   had an aching tooth.
   He never should have
   Visited Doctor Goof!
   _____

6. What's death like?
   says Peter Prank.
   "Blankety-blank-blank
   Blankety-blank."
   _____

7. Here lies Timothy Tate,
   Eaten up by his very
   own hate.
   _____

8. Roger Rumor
   A deadly tumor put him
   In a very bad humor.
   _____

9. Miss Mary Louise
   Caught a very bad disease.
   It made her sneeze
   'Til weak in the knees.
   _____

10. On the way
    To harm a friend,
    Jealous Jason
    Met his end.
    _____

mal

bad

Pardon Me?

Something is not quite right here. For each sentence, cross out the problem word and replace it with the vocabulary word that will make more sense.

1. After several botched surgeries, Dr. Mordred Miles is on trial for medical expertise.

2. Sheila inhaled a deep breath of the fragrant air blowing in from the landfill.

3. Scientists have been studying the puzzling well-being of soldiers exposed to chemical warfare.

4. Muttering angry benedictions, the prisoner shuffled back to his cell.

5. The surgeon was extremely concerned about the benign tumor growing on the young man's arm.

6. For years, people who lived in swampy areas suffered from good air.

7. Her correct words never failed to produce howls of laughter.

8. While the teacher's back was turned, the class bully gave his neighbor a kindly kick in the shins.

9. John Wilkes Booth was the benefactor responsible for Abraham Lincoln's murder.

10. Benevolence is the root of every war.

JUST FOR FUN
See whether you can identify these nursery rhyme characters.

A. What large family lived in a malodorous home?
B. Who received malicious blows for stealing a pig?
C. What pastry chef should have been arrested for malpractice?
D. What malefactor scared a little girl out of her breakfast?

Birthday Blow-out

Cake, candles, presents . . . A birthday party is the greatest—especially if it is yours! All the words below come from the same Latin root, *gen*, meaning "birth" or "origin." Read each definition and match it with the correct *gen* word.

_____ 1. the sex a person is born, male or female
_____ 2. a group of people born around the same time
_____ 3. the children born to a person
_____ 4. born in, growing naturally in a particular region
_____ 5. originating from the one true source
_____ 6. typical of an original, but not coming from the true source
_____ 7. very giving, as if born with plenty of money
_____ 8. a person born with great intelligence
_____ 9. elegant, graceful, as typical of one born to the upper class
_____ 10. the birth or origin of something

a. progeny, n.
b. generous, adj
c. genius, n.
d. gender, n.
e. genteel, adj.
f. generic, adj.
g. generation, n.
h. genesis, n.
i. genuine, adj.
j. indigenous, adj.

Cut around each candle. Fold on the dotted lines so that the candles stand up. With a friend, take turns calling out the vocabulary words. For each correct definition you give, blow out a candle!

gen
birth
origin

Star-Studded Birthday

Ever wonder what a big Hollywood bash is like? Here is your chance to find out! Fill in the missing vocabulary words in the invitation below.

Darling, you are invited to my birthday party!

This bash will be so big, even (1) _____ Californians will be impressed. I will be the talk of Hollywood for three (2) _____!

It does not take a (3) _____ to decide what to bring me. I like (4) _____ diamonds and 14-karat gold. And no (5) _____ gifts please; brand names only! Be (6)_____!

There will be members of each (7) _____ attending the party, so do not park your (8) _____ behavior at home. And no (9) _____ allowed—they only spoil the grown-ups' fun.

Do hope you can make it, Darling!

Love and Kisses,
GiGi

P.S. I may have been around since the (10) _____ of the automobile, but in my heart, I'm 29 forever!

On the back of your paper, answer these questions about GiGi's party. Make certain you use definitions in your answers.

a. Whom does GiGi hope to impress?
b. Describe GiGi's taste. List gifts she likes and tell why.
c. Who is invited to the party? Who may not attend?
d. How should party-goers behave? Why?
e. For how long will people remember GiGi's party? Explain your math.
f. About how old is GiGi? Research your answer.

Kissing Cousins

gen
birth
origin

All the questions below contain words that are related by birth to this week's vocabulary words. They all come from the root *gen*. Try to figure out the meaning of the word as you answer the question. Dictionaries permitted!

1. Where could you go to find information about your genealogy? _____

2. Name a holiday that a Gentile does not celebrate. Why? _____
   _____

3. A horse breeder practices eugenics with two winning race horses. Explain. _____
   _____

4. Who attempted genocide during World War II? Does genocide occur anywhere in the world today? If yes, where? _____
   _____

5. Do you have any famous progenitors? Name any three of your progenitors. _____
   _____

6. If you are a member of the English gentry, what do you inherit? _____
   _____

7. The fortunes of much of the English gentry have degenerated. Why? _____
   _____

8. We call a machine that produces electricity a generator. Why is this name technically incorrect, according to its root meaning? _____
   _____

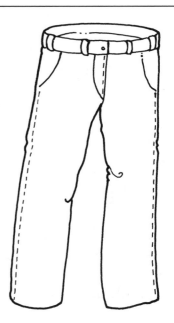

9. Do you have good genes for wearing good jeans? Explain. _____
   _____

10. Name the Mother Goose character who was philoprogenitive. _____

geo, terr
earth

Around the World

Our earth is a fascinating place—especially when you have the right words to describe it. All the words in the puzzle below have *geo* or *terr* as their root, meaning "earth." Read the definition clues and fill in the missing numbers. Hint: The clues are not listed in the correct order.

Across

_____ the physical features of a region of the earth

_____ the sea located in the middle region of the earth

_____ an earth-shaped stone with crystals inside

_____ science that deals with earth's history recorded in rocks

Down

_____ science that records facts about the earth's surface

_____ taking the earth as the center

_____ to bury in the earth

_____ math that deals with the measurement of the earth

_____ lying under the surface of the earth

_____ a level platform of earth

On the back of your paper, write an original sentence of seven words or more for each vocabulary term. When you have finished, check your work. If you left out the vocabulary word, could someone else correctly fill in the blank because of your good sentence? Try it!

Globe Trotters

geo, terr
earth

World travel can certainly enlarge your vocabulary! To play the game below, you will need a stack of cards (one vocabulary word and its meaning per card), two small game markers, and a penny.

Place the cards face down on the desk. To get to move, you must give your partner the correct definition for the word card he/she draws from the stack. If you are right, flip the penny. Heads, you move ahead three spaces; tails, you move one. Then obey the commands on the gameboard. The first person to the finish line is a World-Class Globe Trotter and a vocabulary whiz!

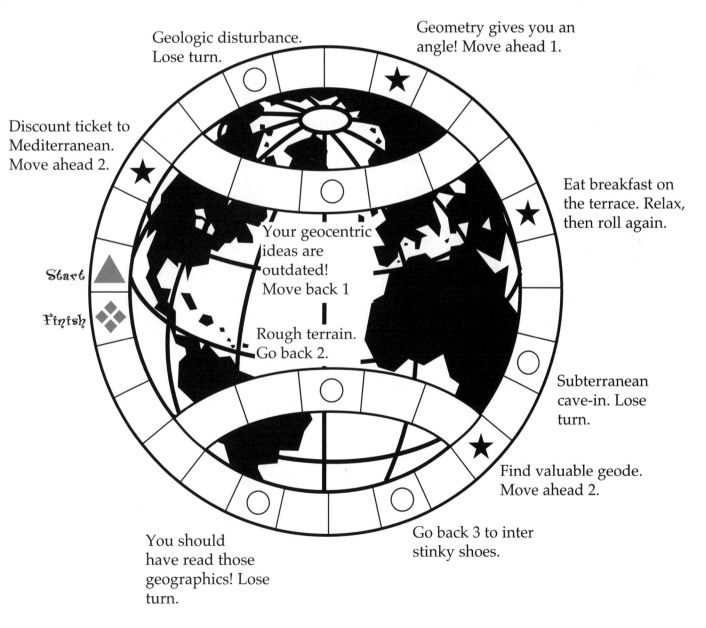

Geologic disturbance. Lose turn.

Geometry gives you an angle! Move ahead 1.

Discount ticket to Mediterranean. Move ahead 2.

Eat breakfast on the terrace. Relax, then roll again.

Your geocentric ideas are outdated! Move back 1

Rough terrain. Go back 2.

Start

Finish

Subterranean cave-in. Lose turn.

Find valuable geode. Move ahead 2.

You should have read those geographics! Lose turn.

Go back 3 to inter stinky shoes.

geo, terr
earth

Where in the World?

All of the vocabulary questions below deal with geography. Use an atlas and an encyclopedia to find the correct answers.

1. In what South American country have hydrolyte geodes been found? _____

2. How did Georgius Agricola further the study of geology? _____

3. How did the ancient Egyptians use geometry? _____

4. Where is the geographic center of North America? _____

5. Who developed ideas that contradicted Ptolemy's geocentric model of the universe?
   _____

6. What famous subterranean tourist site is located in New Mexico? _____

7. Where were Nebuchadnezzar's famous terraced gardens built? _____

8. Where is John F. Kennedy interred? _____

9. Name three Mediterranean countries. _____

10. Describe the terrain of Switzerland. _____

_____

Now turn the tables. Using reference materials, come up with at least three geo/terr questions to stump your teacher. (Hint: Make certain you jot the answers down on a separate sheet of paper before you submit your stumpers.)

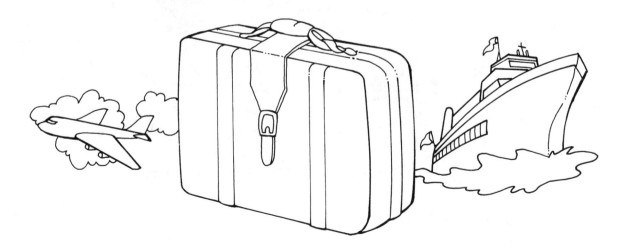

Fancy Footwork

ped, pod
foot

Follow these footprints to vocabulary mastery! The words in the maze below all come from *ped* and *pod*, the Latin roots for "foot." For each step along the way, write in the letter of the correct definition.

a. an insect having many legs
b. a foot lever
c. the support at the foot of a vase or statue
d. a foot traveler
e. care for the feet and toenails
f. an instrument for measuring the distance one covers on foot
g. one who treats disorders of the feet
h. a four-footed animal
i. a three-footed stand
j. an obstacle to one's feet; a hindrance

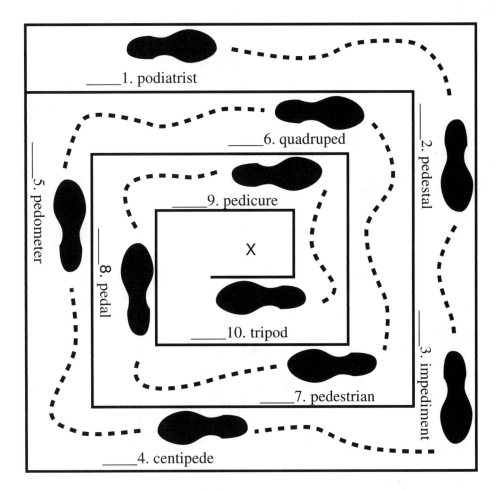

_____1. podiatrist
_____2. pedestal
_____3. impediment
_____4. centipede
_____5. pedometer
_____6. quadruped
_____7. pedestrian
_____8. pedal
_____9. pedicure
_____10. tripod

X

Cut along the bold lines. Attach a length of string at the center X. Hang your fancy footwork where you can review the words frequently.

ped, pod

foot

Feet First

You can jump right into these vocabulary cartoons! For each picture clue, write the most suitable word on the line.

centipede
pedal
pedestal
pedestrian
pedicure
pedometer
podiatrist
quadruped
tripod
impediment

1. _____

2. _____

3. _____

4. _____

5. _____

6. _____

7. _____

8. _____

9. _____

10. _____

Now that you have gotten your feet wet, try drawing your own cartoons for these related words: *octopus, biped, podium.*

© Carson-Dellosa

20

IF87021 Words on the Vine

A Foot in the Door

ped, pod
foot

When it comes to employment, getting your foot in the door means starting at the very bottom. But you never know—that first job might lead to bigger and better things! For each Help Wanted ad below, fill in the missing vocabulary word.

1. Help Wanted: Tough-minded competitor for Olympic bicycle training. Legs must be long enough to reach the _____.
2. Help Wanted: _____ to travel with tap-dancing troupe. Must keep dancers' sore feet in shape through 264 nightly performances.
3. Help Wanted: Cowperson. Must be able to handle huge herds of _____ single-handedly. Roping and yodeling skills optional.
4. Help Wanted: Bulldozer operator to move rocks and other _____ from roads in vicinity of Boulder, Colorado.
5. Help Wanted: Archaeologist has an immediate need for an exterminator experienced in spiders, cockroaches, and _____. All travel expenses to King Tut's tomb paid.
6. Help Wanted: Photographer's assistant to set up cameras and _____. Must have a face that makes people smile.
7. Help Wanted: Museum maintenance worker to dust _____ in Marble Statue Room. No butterfingers need apply.
8. Help Wanted: Quick-thinking salesperson fast on his/her feet for _____ manufacturer.
9. Help Wanted: Animal groomer to work regional dog shows, providing _____ for pampered pooches.
10. Help Wanted: Crossing guard for elementary school. Must be able to control rowdy young _____.

These rhyming riddles will tickle your tootsies! Write the letter of the correct word pair in the blank beside the clue.

_____ 11. a foot doctor with a grateful patient
_____ 12. a chatty pedestrian
_____ 13. a ruined pedicure
_____ 14. a blushing bulldog
_____ 15. an unusual three-legged stand
_____ 16. a multi-legged bug just sprung from jail

a. a red quadruped
b. an odd tripod
c. a walkie-talkie
d. a freed centipede
e. a kissed podiatrist
f. demolished polish

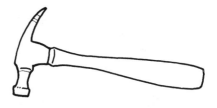

astr, stell
star

Stars and Stripes Forever

These words will shine like stars in your next conversation! They come from the Greek and Latin roots for "star"—*astr* and *stell*. For each definition on the banners below, write the correct star word. Check your answers with a dictionary.

astronomy   astrologer
asteroid   stellar
constellation   aster
stelliform   asterisk
astrodome   disaster

a. _____ a fall flower shaped like a star

b. _____ a group of stars

c. _____ like a star; most important

d. _____ science which studies stars and their movements

e. _____ clear dome of an aircraft for viewing the stars and sky

f. _____ event that occurs under the influence of a negative star; a calamity

g. _____ star-shaped

h. _____ a starlike body in space; a small planet

i. _____ a star used in printing to refer to a margin note

j. _____ person who examines the stars' influence on people

It takes practice for stars to shine their brightest! On the back of your paper, use each vocabulary word in an original sentence of seven words or more.

Twinkle, Twinkle

astr, stell
star

For more than 250 years, Mother Goose rhymes have made bedtime more fun for little children. Here are some wacky new versions of old favorites. Fill in the missing star vocabulary words.

1. Twinkle, twinkle, _____
   Airplane part of glass and chrome.
2. Stars so light, stars so bright,
   First _____ I see tonight.
3. A-tisket, a-tasket,
   An _____ in my trash basket.
   I planned a footnote for the page,
   But when I wrote, I dropped it.
4. Lavender's blue, dilly-dilly,
   _____ are yellow.
   When I am Queen, dilly-dilly,
   You'll be my fellow.
5. Old King Cole was a merry old soul,
   And a merry old soul was he.
   He called for his 'scope for he had great hope
   Of studying _____.
6. Jack and Jill ran down a hill,
   Then started running faster.
   Jill grew ill and took a spill.
   The day was a _____!
7. _____ are falling down,
   Falling down, falling down.
   From outer space right on our town,
   My scared lady.
8. Rub-a-dub-dub, three men in a tub,
   And what _____ fellows
   they be!
   The butcher, the baker, the candlestick maker,
   They made tonight's news on TV!
9. Three little kittens, they lost their mittens,
   So they visited an _____.
   She consulted the stars, found the mittens in jars.
   How gladly those kittens did purr!
10. Patty cake, patty cake, baker's man,
    Bake a _____ cake as fast as you can.
    Ice it silver white and hang it in the sky,
    For Mother Goose to nibble on as she flies by.

Now try your hand at rhyme-writing. Choose any three of this week's vocabulary words and create some up-to-the-minute Mother Goose!

astr, stell

star

Now Playing: Starstomp

Following in the footsteps of Gene Roddenberry and George Lucas, creators of *Star Trek* and *Star Wars*, you're out to make the next blockbuster space movie, *Starstomp*. Answer the questions below to help you with your movie plans. Then write a brief summary of the plot in the space provided. Make certain you include all ten vocabulary words — and may the stars be with you!

1. The setting of *Starstomp* is an experimental colony on an asteroid at the edge of the galaxy. Create a name for the asteroid and tell why the action must take place there.

   _____

2. Homes in the colony are stelliform, with strange purple-green asters growing everywhere. Explain. _____
   _____

3. Approaching the asteroid, the hero of the movie, a starship captain, witnesses a disaster in the corner of the astrodome. Explain. _____
   _____

4. A new constellation is formed because of the disaster. Its creation calls into question the very foundations of astronomy. Why? _____
   _____

5. One of the key characters is an astrologer named Asterisk. How will she figure in the plot? Why is her name significant? _____
   _____

6. What stellar actors will attract viewers to your picture? _____
   _____

Now write your plot here: _____
_____
_____
_____

Clock Wise

Quick! Do not waste another moment! Write the letter for each word beside the matching definition. Check your answers with a dictionary.

a. anachronism
b. chronicles
c. chronic
d. chronometer
e. temporary

f. extemporaneous
g. contemporary
h. tempo
i. synchronize
j. tempest

_____ 1. n., the time of a piece of music, fast or slow

_____ 2. adj., lasting for only a short time

_____ 3. n., anything out of its proper time

_____ 4. n., someone living at the same time

_____ 5. n., a timepiece; a watch; a clock

_____ 6. n., a violent storm lasting for a portion of time

_____ 7. n., a historical account of events of a particular time

_____ 8. v., to cause to happen at the same time

_____ 9. adj., continuing for a long time

_____ 10. adj., given without time to prepare; spur of the moment

chron, temp
time

Beat the Clock

There are at least eight anachronisms in the story below. Number them, and then explain each in the space provided.

It was 1492, and Christopher Columbus and his men were preparing to set sail. "Okay, men, let's synchronize our chronometers," Christopher said over his cellular phone. "We want to weigh anchors at 0800."

Meanwhile, Christopher's contemporaries, Albert Einstein, George Washington, and Moses, stood on the dock shaking their heads. Their friend must be temporarily insane to try such a foolhardy scheme. Should they get him to see a psychiatrist?

But the plucky captain persevered, and his three tiny ships waded out into the Atlantic. To pass the time, sailors danced the hornpipe, tapping out its lively tempo to music blaring from their CD players. Then, to treat the chronic back pain brought on by over-exertion, the men gulped handfuls of aspirin. Suddenly a light on the radar screen flashed. A violent tempest was coming!

Columbus and his ships weathered the storm and landed on San Salvador Island on October 12. As his feet touched the sand, Christopher began a lengthy extemporaneous speech. One of the sailors quietly turned on a tape recorder to preserve his captain's words for future chronicles.

What's wrong with this bit of fractured history? _____

_____

_____

_____

Time Out

chron, temp
time

Time for a little pleasure reading. For each book title listed below, tell what you think the book is all about. Make certain you include the meanings of any time vocabulary words. The first one has been done for you.

1. *The Anachronistic Chick*: The compelling story of a prehistoric hen discovered nesting in the subway of twentieth-century New York City.

2. *Chronicles of a Chronic Complainer* _____

   _____

3. *Collectible Chronometers* _____

   _____

4. *Making Tantrums Temporary* _____

   _____

5. *Modern Warfare: The Contemporary Tank* _____

   _____

6. *Synchronized Sipping* _____

   _____

7. *The Extemporaneous Expert* _____

   _____

8. *Tampa Tempo* _____

   _____

9. *Battling Tide and Tempest* _____

   _____

Now let's turn the tables. For each of the descriptions below, make up a catchy title.
A. The story of a spoiled child who throws a fit every time the weather gets bad:

   _____

B. How to give a memorable farewell speech on the spur of the moment:_____

   _____

C. The globe-trotting adventures of a clock-fancier: _____

   _____

Wet and Wonderful!

Get your feet wet with these water words. They all contain either the root *aqua* or the root *hydr*, from the Latin and Greek words for "water."

Test your memory! Cut out all the squares and place them face down on a table. How many pairs can you correctly match? Next, write the letter of the correct definition drop on each faucet. Check your answers with a dictionary.

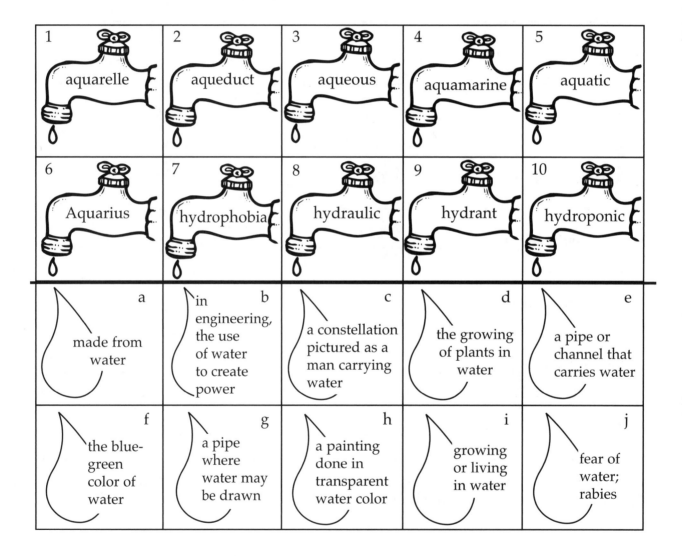

1 aquarelle	2 aqueduct	3 aqueous	4 aquamarine	5 aquatic
6 Aquarius	7 hydrophobia	8 hydraulic	9 hydrant	10 hydroponic

a made from water	b in engineering, the use of water to create power	c a constellation pictured as a man carrying water	d the growing of plants in water	e a pipe or channel that carries water
f the blue-green color of water	g a pipe where water may be drawn	h a painting done in transparent water color	i growing or living in water	j fear of water; rabies

Tanks a Lot!

The Vocabulary Aquarium is unlike any you have ever seen before!
Follow the instructions to draw in these unique features.

1. The water is aquamarine.
2. Tiny aquatic animals gather in one corner.
3. A fish in sick bay suffers from hydrophobia.
4. An octopus makes aquarelles for tourists to take home.
5. The aquarium is supplied by an aqueduct powered by a hydraulic pump.
6. Two fish are busily engaged in hydroponics.
7. State law requires a hydrant on the premises.
8. Aquarius shines in the sky over the aquarium.
9. There is a booth selling aqueous refreshments next door.

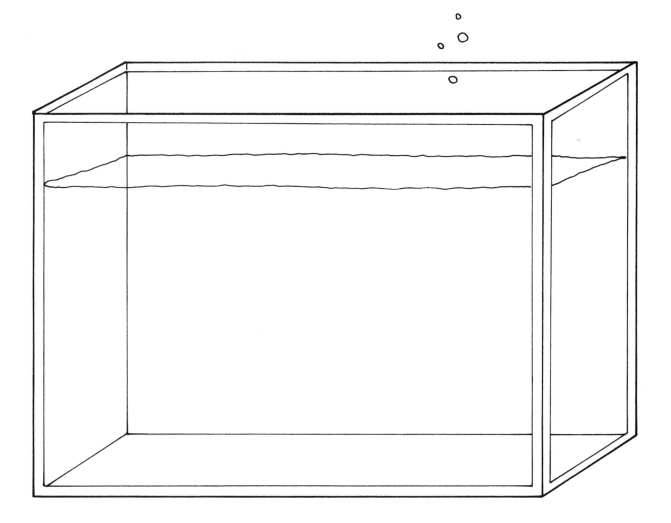

How did people keep track of time in the days before analog clocks and watches? Fill in the blanks below with water vocabulary to find out.

"Endless arguments about the new (1) _____ system powering the
(2) _____ that brings water into Athens.... Complaints about
(3) _____ canines loose in the streets... Motions to raise money for new
(4) _____ for the art museum..."

It was the year 435 B.C., and the great thinker Plato looked disgusted as he sat muttering to himself.

"Words pour from our politicians' mouths like water from a (5) _____! I spend all my time here in the Senate instead of doing important things such as (6) _____ gardening. There must be some way to set a time limit for each speaker."

The philosopher stared up at (7) _____ high in the night sky. His (8) _____ eyes suddenly lit up with inspiration.

"Eureka! I think I've come up with an (9) _____ solution to the problem! I'll invent an (10) _____ clock! I will make a hole in a large glass jar which has a series of marks on its side. Then I will fill the jar with water. Each senator may speak until the water level drops from one mark to the next. Then he must sit down."

"Lily pads, here I come!"

11. What was Plato's hobby? _____

12. What were some of the problems plaguing Athens? _____
_____

13. Describe the Athenian senators._____
_____

14. How did Plato get his good idea? _____
_____

Although the monologue above is imaginary, Plato is credited with inventing the first water clock, also known as a *clepsydra*. Use an encyclopedia to research further developments made on this early timepiece.

Power Under the Hood

mob, mot
move

The root words *mob* and *mot* come from the Latin, meaning "to move." Combined with different prefixes, these roots give us many words dealing with motion—true power under the hood!

Ladies and gentlemen, start your engines. For each prefix and definition below, find a matching root from the Pit Stop. Cross it off as you use it.

1. pro   +_____ = v., to move forward in position or authority

2. com   +_____ = n., disturbing noise and movement

3. de   +_____ = v., to move down in position or authority

4. e   +_____ = n., strong inner movement, feeling

5. im   +_____ = adj., unable to move

6. re   +_____ = adj., distant

7. loco   +_____ = n., power to move from place to place

8. auto   +_____ = n., vehicle capable of moving on its own

9. un   +_____ = adj., not prompted to move or act

10. non   +_____ = adj., not capable of spontaneous movement

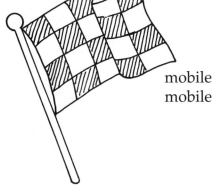

Pit Stop

mobile	mote	motion	motile
mobile	mote	motion	motivated
	mote	motion	

Even winning race car drivers need practice. On the back of your paper, write a sentence of seven or more words for each vocabulary term. Use driving as your topic.

mob, mot
move

Motion City

The warnings and directions given here belong somewhere on the map of Motion City below. For each one, draw a circle in the correct spot and label with the matching sign number.

1. Proceed with Caution
   Commotion Ahead

2. Demoted Motorists
   Check-in

3. Promotion Day Today

4. Nonmotivated Students
   Sleep Here

5. On Sale Today
   Emotion Potion

6. Remote Hideaways
   Turn Right

7. Nonmobile Automobiles
   Park Here

8. Immobilized Flies
   Enter Here

9. Locomotive Luggage
   Claim

Add three places of your own to the Motion City map, complete with motion vocabulary signs.

Motion Sickness

mob, mot

move

What do you call a cool motion picture from the 60s? A groovy movie!
Hold on to your hat—this riddle ride gets really wild! For each clue below, write the
letter of the correct answer.

_____ 1. a distant ship

_____ 2. rough seas

_____ 3. an unmotivated flower

_____ 4. the primary locomotive

_____ 5. a duke in a cast

_____ 6. a bottled automobile

_____ 7. ad campaign for skin softener

_____ 8. boss's idea to lower an employee's status

_____ 9. a cheerleader's emotion

A. lotion promotion
B. the main train
C. a car in a jar
D. a squealing feeling
E. a lazy daisy
F. a demotion notion
G. a remote boat
H. immobile noble
I. ocean in commotion

ACTING UP - With a partner, plan a pantomime for each motion vocabulary word. See
whether classmates can guess which word you are depicting.

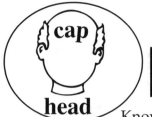

cap

head

Head Hunters

Knowing vocabulary roots can keep you out of hot water! All the words appearing below share the root *cap*, meaning "head." Write the letter of each word beside the matching definition. Check your answers with a dictionary.

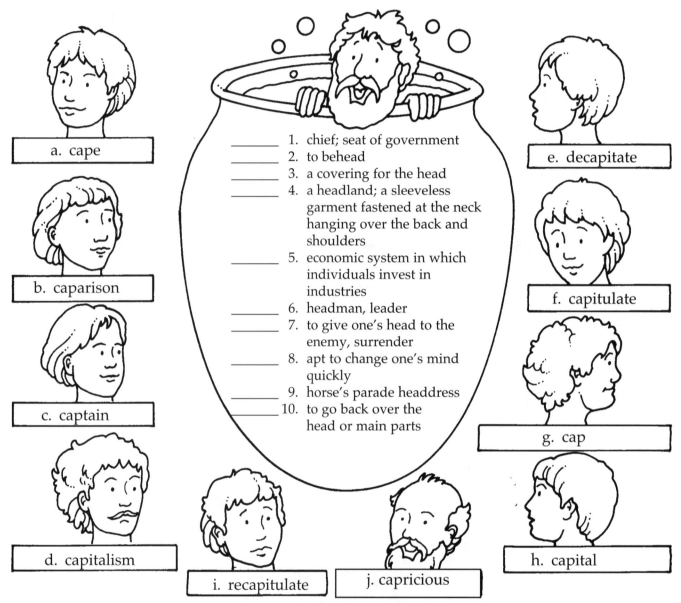

a. cape

b. caparison

c. captain

d. capitalism

e. decapitate

f. capitulate

g. cap

h. capital

i. recapitulate

j. capricious

_____ 1. chief; seat of government
_____ 2. to behead
_____ 3. a covering for the head
_____ 4. a headland; a sleeveless garment fastened at the neck hanging over the back and shoulders
_____ 5. economic system in which individuals invest in industries
_____ 6. headman, leader
_____ 7. to give one's head to the enemy, surrender
_____ 8. apt to change one's mind quickly
_____ 9. horse's parade headdress
_____ 10. to go back over the head or main parts

Don't keep those new words bottled up in your head! Put them to work. Finish this headline-making story. Use all ten vocabulary words.

The missionary gulped as he noticed the large assortment of knives hanging on the wall of the hut. "Don't worry, sir," the chief grinned. "We don't decapitate our guests, we . . . ."

Upper Case Code

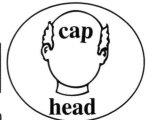

The Upper Case Code was invented in the fifteenth century by Italian architect and code expert Leon Battista Alberti. Spies on both sides in the American Civil War used it to relay information back to their headquarters.

Now it's your turn. In the outer ring below, fill in the upper case alphabet starting with A and moving clockwise. This completed wheel is your key to cracking the coded vocabulary sentences below!

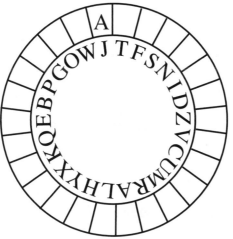

1. QZN FJHVQJM LI ANP CNXKNO VK QXNAQLA.

2. FLEMS KEHNXRJA IMO PVQZLEQ ZVK FJHN?

3. "ANBNX FJHVQEMJQN!" KZLEQNS DNANXJM FEKQNX.

4. KZEQQMN QL AJKJ: XNFJHVQEMJQN KJINQO XEMNK JKJH!

5. FJHQJVA FZJXMNK MVASTNXDZ RJSN ZVK IJRLEK IMVDZQ VA 1927.

6. "MNRLAJSN ILX KJMN," FJMMNS QZN CEAVLX FJHVQJMVKQ.

7. QZN YENNA LI ZNJXQK PJAQNS QL SNFJHVQJQN JMVFN.

8. XNRLBVAD LAN'K FJH KZLPK XNKHNFQ.

9. IVFUMN VK J KOALAOR ILX FJHXVFVLEK.

10. PZJQ'K J HJXJSN PVQZLEQ FJHJXVKLANS ZLXKNK?

Now use the Upper Case Code to send a secret message to a friend. Write a sentence in code that contains any two "cap" words.

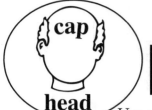

History/Mysteries

Use your expertise in vocabulary to solve the History/Mysteries below. You may use any reference materials you wish to locate answers.

1. Famous Texas conflict in which Jim Bowie and Davy Crockett refused to capitulate:

   _____

2. Arthur's hand-picked warriors, whose horses wore different identifying caparisons:

   _____

3. Decapitation device used during the French Revolution: _____

4. Dangerous South American headland around which whaling ships of the 1880s dreaded sailing:_____

5. Famous English document of 1215 in which noblemen recapitulated their demand for rights: _____

6. Economic system currently replacing communism in former Soviet countries:

   _____

7. Leader of Jamestown settlers, rescued by Pocahontas:_____

8. American armed conflict in which troops on both sides wore flat caps called *kepis:*

   _____

9. Capricious English king who tired of five of his six wives:_____

10. Capital of the American Colonies during most of the Revolutionary War: _____

Now write three History/Mysteries of your own, using "head" vocabulary words. See if your teacher can get the correct answers!

His and Hers

mater, pater

mother, father

Here's one family that knows what's his and what's hers! The words on the doors below come from the Latin and Greek roots for "mother" and "father," *mater* and *pater*. First, cut out the definition squares at the bottom of the page. Then cut around each door, following the dotted lines. Glue the correct definition on the back side of each open door.

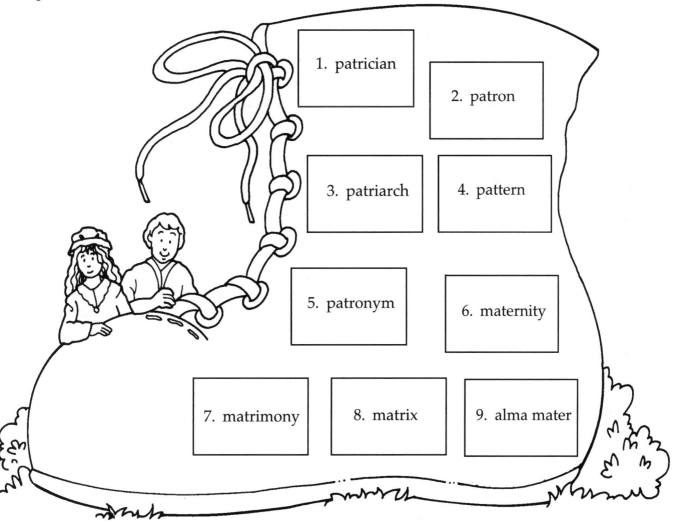

1. patrician

2. patron

3. patriarch

4. pattern

5. patronym

6. maternity

7. matrimony

8. matrix

9. alma mater

a. the place where mothering occurs; womb	b. male head of a family	c. a model worthy of copying, like a father	d. fostering mother, school	e. a name taken from one's father
f. person of high birth, as descending from founding fathers	g. marrying a woman to make her a mother	h. motherhood	i. a supporter, like one's father	

37

mater, pater

mother, father

Family Matters

Family stories make the newspapers every day. Here are some wacky headlines using mother/father vocabulary words. For each one, write a first sentence telling what you think the story is about. You may use a dictionary if you wish.

1. Poisoned Pork Patties Paralyze Pushy Patrician

_____

_____

2. Pickle Patrons Pester Pope with Picnic Parcels

_____

_____

3. "Hark, a Stark Bark in the Park!" remarks Patriarch Quark _____

_____

4. Pittsburgh Zoo Our Otter Alma Mater _____

_____

5. Must Maternity Seem Like Eternity? _____

_____

6. No Baloney—Phony Matrimony, Says County Clerk of Records _____

_____

7. "Full to Brim of Patronyms," Say Jim, Jim, and Jim _____

_____

8. New Mother Finds Matrix, Politics Don't Mix _____

_____

9. Peppy Painter Puts Panda Pattern on Paper Panties _____

_____

Now it's your turn! On the back, write three wacky headlines of your own, using this week's vocabulary words.

All in the Family

mater, pater
mother, father

Mater/pater words fill a large family tree. Use a dictionary to check the meanings of these related words and answer the questions.

1. Are all matrons required to be matronly-looking? Explain. _____
   _____

2. Which would you rather have right now—matrimony or a patrimony? Why?
   _____
   _____

3. Name your family's matriarch (you may have more than one). What are the
   qualifications for the job? _____
   _____

4. Into what mothering organization have you matriculated? Explain. _____
   _____

5. Do all men participating in paternity have paternal instincts? Why or why not?
   _____
   _____

6. What is the difference between patronizing your favorite store and patronizing your
   little brother? _____
   _____

7. What would your name be if your family had matronymic inclinations? Explain.
   _____
   _____

8. When a patriot sings, "America," which is his favorite line? Why?
   _____
   _____

9. Do all matriculants wear a cap and gown? Explain. _____
   _____

Goody Goody Gumdrops

Are you ready for a treat? Then master these words that contain *bene* or *bon*, roots meaning "good." Write the letter of the matching definition under each vocabulary word. Check your answers with a dictionary. Next, cover each answer with a small piece of real candy. Now review your words. For each correct answer you give, reward yourself with—what else?—a bonbon!

a. good words, blessing
b. an extra reward for goodness
c. in good faith, genuine
d. good-doing; kind
e. gentle, good, harmless
f. good and plentiful
g. one who gives good things
h. one who receives good things
i. good, rich ore deposit, anything yielding abundance
j. a lover of good living, especially food

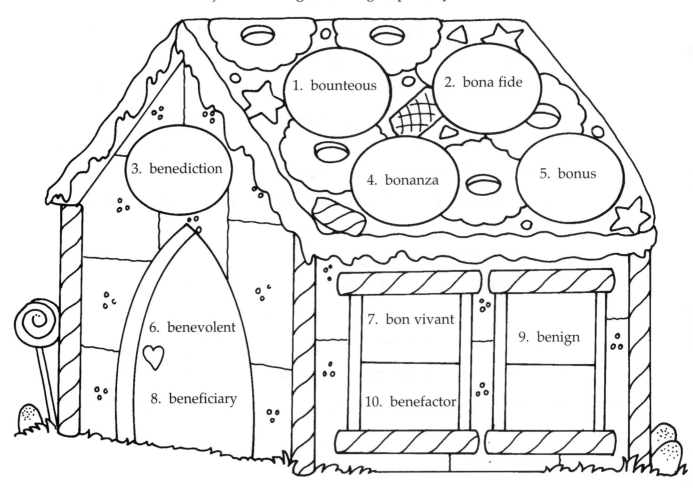

1. bounteous
2. bona fide
3. benediction
4. bonanza
5. bonus
6. benevolent
7. bon vivant
8. beneficiary
9. benign
10. benefactor

Bon Voyage

The sentences below are from A-1 Travel, an agency that plans tours to the world's most exciting destinations. Fill in each blank with the correct vocabulary word.

When you travel with A-1, you go with style and confidence!

All our employees are (1) _____ travel experts, trained to help you experience the peak of touring pleasure. You will be the (2) _____ of their years of knowledge and proficiency. Before every tour begins, our leaders give a (3) _____ asking for the blessings of health and safety for all. And the food—each meal on your A-1 trip will be a (4) _____ feast, the very finest and freshest of all the good earth has to offer. We are currently accepting reservations for the following tours:

> The Last Chance Rain Forest—Hurry, see one of the last spots on earth untouched by trash and pollution. Prospectors searching for emeralds struck a (5) _____ of pure gold here in 1898—and kept the secret for years!

> Feed'n'Read Tour—Designed for bookworms and (6) _____, this trip features the greatest libraries and restaurants in Europe. After a hard day's reading, you'll get to see famous chefs at work, chopping, dicing, slicing, shouting, giving orders—(7) _____ dictators of their culinary kingdoms.

> Lizard Island—They look ferocious, but in reality the giant lizards on this remote island are (8) _____, simply content to eat and sleep in the sun. Once endangered, they are now protected by their (9) _____, the reclusive millionaire who owns the island. Maybe you will be the first to spot him!

So book your trip with A-1 Travel today and, as a (10) _____ for signing up early, we will send you, at absolutely no cost, this personalized disposable air sickness bag. Yours free with your paid-in-full reservation. Happy traveling!

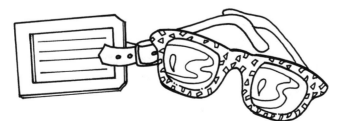

bene, bon
good

For Goodness' Sake

Use your knowledge of vocabulary to identify these special people and special days.

1. The benefactor who brings down chimneys.

2. *Bon vivant's* dream, with turkey, potatoes, and pie.

3. He set the example, giving benedictions and financial aid; today we give hearts, candy, and flowers.

4. Looking only for spice, he discovered a bonanza of forests, rivers, animals, and minerals instead.

5. Bringer of bounteous baskets containing goodies and eggs.

6. Benign little ghosts and goblins beg for bonbons.

7. We are the beneficiaries of his efforts to bring equality to all races.

8. Little people who lure big people away from bona fide trails of gold.

9. Benevolent founding fathers' birthday.

10. Bonus day, occurring one out of four.

Now put those new words to work yourself. Write vocabulary clues for each of the following holidays:

11. Arbor Day _____

12. Fourth of July _____

13. Labor Day _____

14. Hanukkah _____

15. Veterans' Day _____

Play Ball!

ject, jet
throw

Cut out the pitcher's arm below and attach it at the X with a metal fastener. Turn the arm to make ten correct *ject/jet* words. You will discover they all have something to do with "throwing." Check your answers with a dictionary.

1. in + _____ + ion n., the throwing of medicine into flesh by a needle

2. e + _____ v., to throw out

3. _____ + tison v., to throw goods overboard to lighten

(pitcher's arm illustration: ject, jet   X)

4. sub + _____ v., to throw under another's power

5. de + _____ + ion n., a feeling of being thrown down in spirit

6. tra + _____ + ory n., the curved path of an object thrown into space

7. re + _____ n., an object thrown out because it is defective

8. pro + _____ + ion n., a long-range plan thrown out for analysis and discussion

9. inter + _____ + ion n., a word thrown into a sentence or conversation

10. pro + _____ + ile n., an object thrown into the air with great force

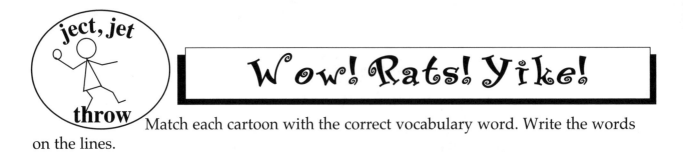

Wow! Rats! Yike!

Match each cartoon with the correct vocabulary word. Write the words on the lines.

reject

projection

projectile

eject

trajectory

interjections

jettison

injection

subjects

dejection

1. _____

2. _____

3. _____

4. _____

5. _____

6. _____

7. _____

8. _____

9. _____

10. _____

44

Flotsam and Jetsam

ject, jet
throw

Flotsam and *jetsam* are nautical terms that refer to things a sailor might throw overboard—trash, heavy cargo, the captain. Here's a scavenger hunt for the flotsam and jetsam you find at school. Fill in the blanks with vocabulary words, then split into teams and play the game.

1. Find five homework assignments with answers that have been _____.

2. Make a paper _____. Prove that it really works.

3. Name three behaviors that would get you _____ from school.

4. Launch an empty milk carton outside. Estimate the _____.

5. For what communicable diseases do teachers at your school get _____? Survey three different teachers.

6. _____ the trash from your bookbag into a paper bag. Present it with a smile to your favorite teacher.

7. Locate a texture with _____ on it.

8. List as many G-rated _____ as you can.

9. Interview the happiest person you know. Find out when he/she last felt _____ and why.

10. List the _____ to which all students in your grade must _____ themselves in order to be promoted at the end of the year.

Now write ten new scavenger clues using this week's vocabulary words. Make them as different from the ones above as possible. Play the game again.

Marshmallows, Please

flam, pyro
fire

Here's how to have a hot time—master words that contain *flam* and *pyro*, the roots for "fire"! On each match word below, write the letter of the correct definition. Check your answers with a dictionary.

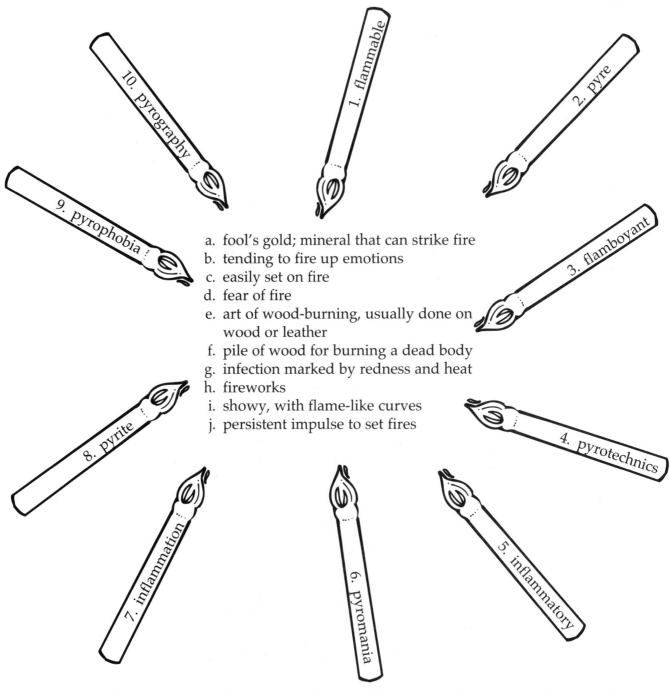

10. pyrography

1. flammable

2. pyre

9. pyrophobia

3. flamboyant

8. pyrite

4. pyrotechnics

7. inflammation

6. pyromania

5. inflammatory

a. fool's gold; mineral that can strike fire
b. tending to fire up emotions
c. easily set on fire
d. fear of fire
e. art of wood-burning, usually done on wood or leather
f. pile of wood for burning a dead body
g. infection marked by redness and heat
h. fireworks
i. showy, with flame-like curves
j. persistent impulse to set fires

Can you light a campfire with three matches or less? It takes practice! On the back of your paper, write a sentence of seven or more words for each vocabulary term. Use camping as your topic.

International House of Heartburn

Welcome to Pyrosis Palace, otherwise known as the International House of Heartburn. To learn about tonight's specials, fill in the blanks with the missing vocabulary words.

Our specials of the evening include:

-Twelve Alarm Chili. Never fear, it's not (1)_____, but it is guaranteed to cure head colds and (2)_____ of all sorts.

-(3)_____ Ham. A dish so delicious, angry emotions will break out at your table over who gets the last bite.

-(4)_____ Potatoes. We call this "Fool's Gold," chunks of Idaho potatoes floating like nuggets in a unique golden sauce made from 27 top secret ingredients.

-Chilly Beet Soup. Not one degree of heat has interfered with the earth's natural goodness. From the field to the blender straight to your bowl. Slurped by (5)_____ all over town.

The evening concludes with dessert. The culinary (6)_____ include:

-Baked Alaska. Dished up by singing waiters and violins, for those who appreciate life's little (7)_____ flourishes.

-Pumpkin (8)_____. A generous puff of creamy pumpkin atop a pile of chocolate "logs." A dying man would wish for this!

-Bananas Flambé. Flaming fruit on a stick for the (9)_____.

So come visit us soon! Look for the big sign with our name written in (10) _____ _____. We'll turn up the heat for you—and that's a promise!

Snap, Crackle, Pop!

Light up the sky with some fireworks! Read each sentence below and decide whether the vocabulary word is used correctly. If it is, draw fireworks in the margin. Rewrite any incorrect sentences to show how to use the vocabulary words properly.

1. Because of his young son's problem with pyromania, Mr. Marshall allowed no matches or lighters in the house.

2. The gang leader, gifted with inflammatory speech, could stir his members to angry action with just a word or two.

3. After the tragic deaths of several children, Congress passed a law requiring that all pajamas be made from flammable fabric.

4. In ancient India, it was the custom for a wife to jump into her dead husband's funeral pyre.

5. He liked cooking his vegetables in pyrite because the clear glass dish was heat-resistant.

6. Pyrography, a Japanese art form, is done with rice paper, black ink, and soft brushes.

7. As the queen approached the muddy street, Sir Walter Raleigh flung his cape on the ground in a flamboyant gesture.

8. It took two days for the team of pyrotechnic experts to set up the Fourth of July extravaganza.

9. The original wound made by the knife was not severe, but when inflammation set in, Joe's arm began to hurt.

10. The pyrophobe eagerly grabbed a stick and stirred the campfire into a roaring inferno.

Blue Ribbon Specials

prim, prin, proto

1

first

You deserve a medal for vocabulary mastery! The words below all come from *prim*, *prin*, and *proto*, the roots meaning "first" or "basic." For each word, write the letter of the matching definition. Check your answers with a dictionary.

- a. belonging to the first years
- b. first, most important, most basic
- c. most important female opera singer
- d. first book, elementary reading book
- e. first-born son of a king
- f. territory belonging to a son of a king
- g. a basic truth
- h. rules governing government ceremonies
- i. the first, most important character in a book or play
- j. first ancestor

Now have some fun with your new words. Cut out the medals and award them to your friends. Tape each medal on a classmate and make a brief presentation speech using the vocabulary word: "Jack, for your role as protagonist in last week's game against Laney Middle School, I present you with this medal."

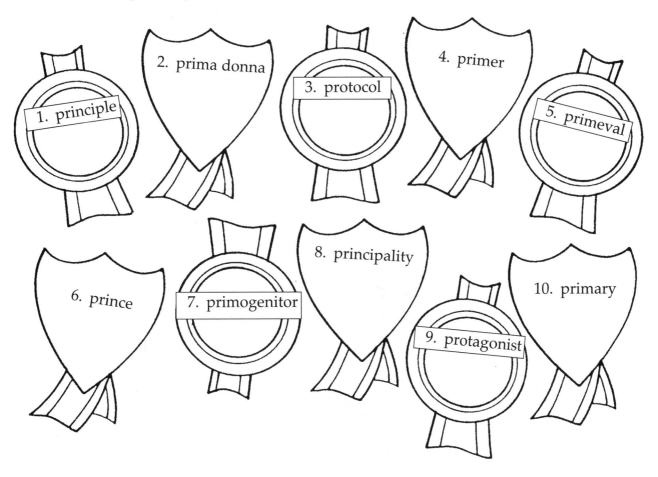

1. principle
2. prima donna
3. protocol
4. primer
5. primeval
6. prince
7. primogenitor
8. principality
9. protagonist
10. primary

prim, prin, proto

1

first

The Princess and the Pea

Hidden in the fairy tale below are the definitions for your ten "first" vocabulary words. Read the story and underline definitions as you come to them. Over each one, write the matching vocabulary word.

"What will we do?" sighed the old queen. "We will never find a suitable wife for the son of the king. We must follow strict rules about government ceremonies to locate the right young woman for the job."

"Of first, most basic importance are her first ancestors. We need to trace them back to the very first era. Over what countries or territories belonging to king's sons have they ruled? Only a princess of many generations is good enough to marry my son!"

"Secondly, we must consider the young lady's basic beliefs and education. Has she progressed past the first reading book level? It takes brains and character to be a queen. The final test involves placing a green pea under the main character's mattress. If she is a true pampered, prissy woman, every inch of her body will ache the next day!"

Now write this story from the young lady's point of view. How did she feel sleeping on a lumpy mattress? Use all ten vocabulary words in your monologue.

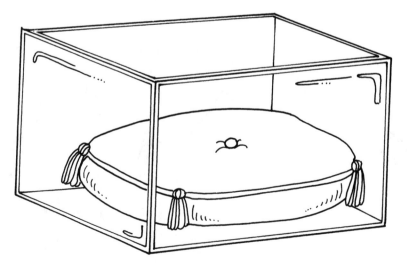

First Impressions

prim, prin, proto
1
first

After designers sketch an idea for a new coin, they make a prototype, a first model which they refine and shape and get just right. Then a mold is made and the assembly line cranked up. The first new coin out of the mold is called a *first impression*. If you can get your hands on one, it is usually worth much more than the face value of the coin.

Use your knowledge of the *prim*/*proto* roots to answer the following questions.

1. Write protocol for dealing with a prima donna.

2. Were primates present during primeval times?

3. When would a prince need a primer?

4. Give a list of ten principles for principals.

5. What quality do prime numbers have in common with primary colors?

6. Who currently governs the principality of Monaco?

7. Why do some scientists believe that dinosaurs were the primogenitors of the modern bird?

8. Name the protagonist and his antagonists from your favorite movie.

9. Plan the prototype for a twenty-first-century primer. Describe it here.

10. Explain what a presidential primary is.

rota, volv
turn

Making Tracks

These words will really make your wheels spin! They all come from the Latin and Greek words for "turn"—*rota* and *volv*. For each word, write the letter of the matching definition on the blank. Check your answers with a dictionary.

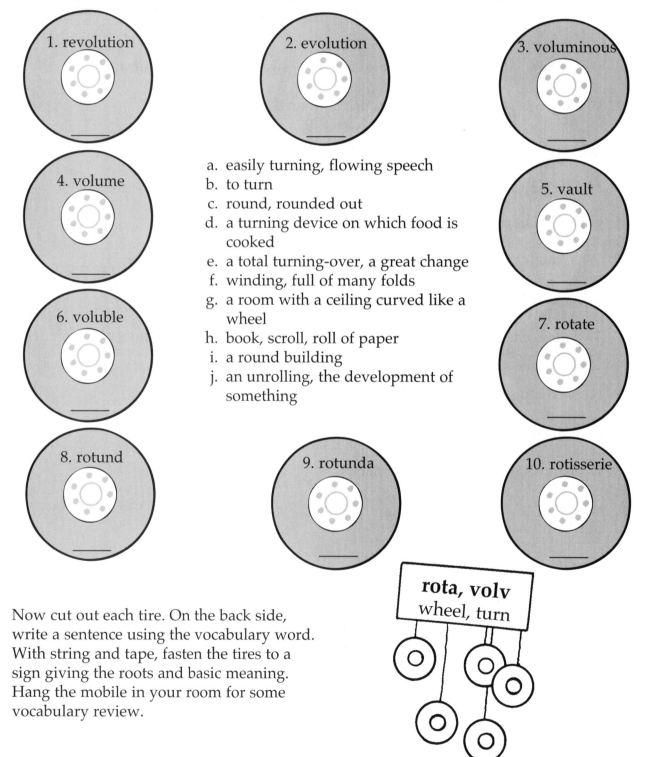

1. revolution

2. evolution

3. voluminous

4. volume

5. vault

a. easily turning, flowing speech
b. to turn
c. round, rounded out
d. a turning device on which food is cooked
e. a total turning-over, a great change
f. winding, full of many folds
g. a room with a ceiling curved like a wheel
h. book, scroll, roll of paper
i. a round building
j. an unrolling, the development of something

6. voluble

7. rotate

8. rotund

9. rotunda

10. rotisserie

rota, volv
wheel, turn

Now cut out each tire. On the back side, write a sentence using the vocabulary word. With string and tape, fasten the tires to a sign giving the roots and basic meaning. Hang the mobile in your room for some vocabulary review.

Wheel of Fortune

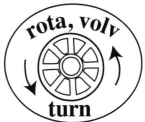

Congratulations! You are the big winner on a TV game show. Now it is time to spin the prize wheel. You will need a small paper clip and a pencil. Place the paper clip at the center of the wheel. Use your pencil point to hold the clip in place as you give it a spin.

Write the prize number on your paper and explain what you plan to do with your prize. Spin until everything on the wheel is yours!

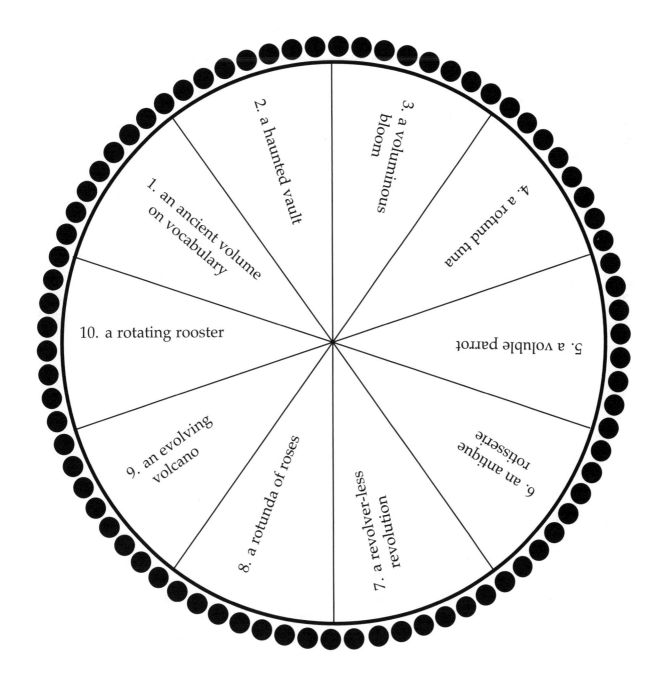

rota, volv
turn

In the Pit

The bubbles below contain comments overheard at the hottest conversation pit in town. Write the letter of the bubble in the blank beside the correct speaker.

a. I'll take a fifth helping, please. I must maintain my rotund figure.

b. No corners to get dusty in here!

c. I turn them and burn them and serve them up hot!

d. We must turn everything upside down.

e. Have you ever tried sitting in one of these?

f. No vacancies in this vault!

g. This started out as a story but it evolved into a play.

h. These volumes are so rare that we keep them locked up.

i. It helps to have the gift of gab.

j. I calculate the speed of the earth's rotations.

_____ 1. -said a woman wearing a voluminous skirt.

_____ 2. -said a librarian.

_____ 3. -said a voluble salesperson.

_____ 4. -said a maintenance man at the Capitol rotunda.

_____ 5. -said a crowd of corpses.

_____ 6. -said a Japanese sumo wrestler.

_____ 7. -said a rotisserie chef.

_____ 8. -said a writer.

_____ 9. -said a soldier in the American Revolution.

_____ 10. -said a scientist.

Heartbroken

cor
heart

Don't cry! With a little loving care and a good vocabulary, this heart will mend. Each word on the list below contains the Latin root for "heart," *cor*. Look for the matching definition on the broken pieces and write the word in the blank.

accord   courage
accordion   cordial
discord   encourage
concord   discourage
concordance   record

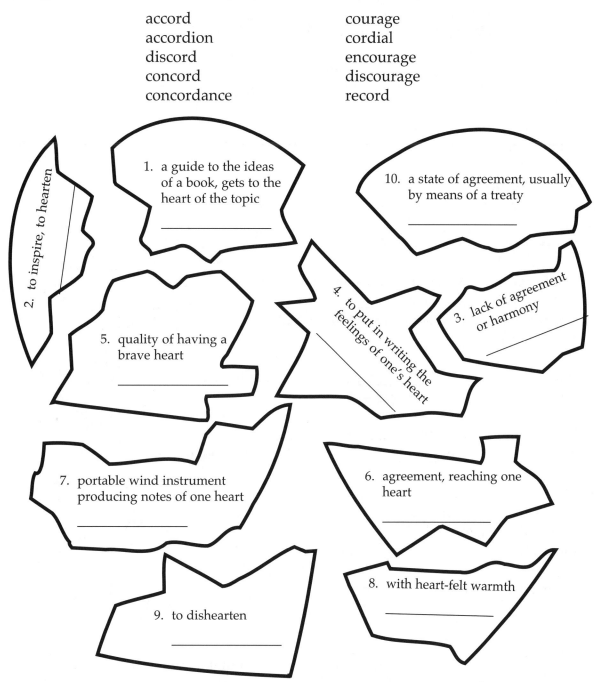

2. to inspire, to hearten

1. a guide to the ideas of a book, gets to the heart of the topic
_____

10. a state of agreement, usually by means of a treaty
_____

5. quality of having a brave heart
_____

4. to put in writing the feelings of one's heart
_____

3. lack of agreement or harmony
_____

7. portable wind instrument producing notes of one heart
_____

6. agreement, reaching one heart
_____

8. with heart-felt warmth
_____

9. to dishearten
_____

Now cut along the bold lines and put this heart back together. Glue the pieces to a sheet of construction paper and look over your words until you know them—by heart!

55

cor

heart

Love Letters

There are thousands of ways to say, "I love you." Ten of them are given below. Your job is to read each love letter and fill in the missing vocabulary word.

1. Valentine, my heart's like an _____.
   Squeeze it and it will make heart-felt harmonies for you!

2. Your smiles _____ me.
   Am I right in thinking that you'll be my Valentine?

3. Valentine, I'm scared and shy.
   It takes all my _____ just to say, "Hi."

4. It's now official, Valentine!
   This Treaty of Love proclaims
   That a state of _____
   Exists between the two of us!

5. Listen carefully, Valentine, and you'll hear that
   Our hearts beat with one _____.

6. The book of my love for you is so huge, Valentine,
   You'll need a _____!

7. Put this in the _____ book, Valentine.
   I'm the world's greatest lover—of you!

8. I'm sorry, Valentine. It's time to make peace.
   There should be no _____ between you and me.

9. Here's some cake, here's some pie,
   Here's some cookies, too.
   Valentine, can you tell—
   I feel very _____ towards you?

10. No more frowns please, Valentine.
    It's too _____.

Now choose three of your favorite sayings above and make them into Valentine cards. Make certain that your illustrations match the meanings of the words.

By Heart

cor

heart

Each of the history/mysteries below has some connection with the heart. Use reference materials to locate the answers.

1. Who invented the accordion in 1829? By what other name is this instrument known?
   _____

2. The most commonly available concordances are written to aid students in research of a world-famous book of faith. Name the book._____

3. Explain why the supersonic transport built by England and France was named the *Concorde.*_____
   _____

4. What war is described in the famous book *The Red Badge of Courage*? _____

5. Many adults say much of today's rock music is discordant. Explain._____
   _____

6. The first sound recording was made on tin-wrapped cylinders that could be played on a phonograph. Who invented this process? _____ When?_____

7. What famous chemist, after inventing dynamite, went on to use his earnings to found an international prize promoting world accord? _____

8. There are several authors famous for their guides to cordial behavior. Name any one of them._____

9. What two books encouraged young Abraham Lincoln in his boyhood on the Indiana frontier? _____

10. Who discouraged Florence Nightingale from a career in nursing and why?_____
    _____
    _____

Now write three history/mysteries of your own, using *heart* vocabulary words. See whether your classmates can get the correct answers!

rect, reg

king

Tyrannosaurus Rex

His name tells us he was the king of the prehistoric world, but Tyrannosaurus Rex ruled only in the final days of the Mesozoic Era. Words, on the other hand, can reign forever!

All the words in the puzzle below have *rect* or *reg* as their root, meaning "king" or "right ruler." Read the definition clues and fill in the missing numbers. (Hint: The clues are not listed in the correct order.)

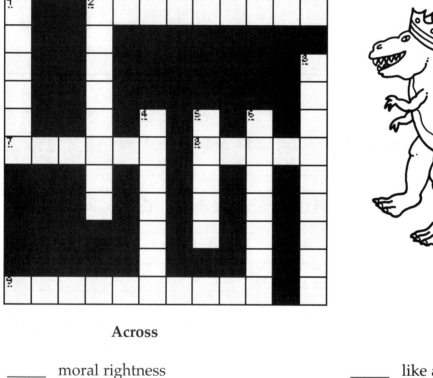

Across

_____ moral rightness

_____ the manner of a ruler's government

_____ upright, not leaning

_____ a law made by a ruler

Down

_____ like a king

_____ the fancy clothing of a king

_____ a routine of right habits

_____ the murder of a king

_____ a right-angled parallelogram

_____ the ruler of a church

On the back of your paper, write an original sentence of seven words or more for each vocabulary term. Give your sentences a prehistoric setting!

Nestor, Court Jester

rect, reg
king

Nestor's job was to keep King Midas laughing. Here are some of Nestor's "golden-oldies." Write the letter of the correct answer beside each riddle.

_____ 1. a regimen of frequent baths and showers

_____ 2. a rectangular grizzly

_____ 3. a regicide weapon

_____ 4. rule by Baskin Robbins

_____ 5. an inherited tendency to stand erect

_____ 6. the king of birds

_____ 7. regalia for playing a board game with knights and pawns

_____ 8. regulation for kittens

_____ 9. a rector known for quick sermons

_____ 10. a cannibal's favorite meal of moral missionary

a. the ice cream regime

b. stewed rectitude

c. a regal eagle

d. the faster pastor

e. bear in a square

f. claw law

g. a clean routine

h. the straight trait

i. the thing that zinged the king

j. chess dress

Once King Midas stopped laughing at Nestor's crazy riddles, he grew thoughtful. Was there real sense and wisdom hiding behind Nestor's silliness? The king pulled his jester into a private chamber. "I know these riddles must be clues about something dangerous to my kingdom. Explain yourself, Nestor!"

Choose five of the riddles above and tell how they are clues to the secret plot Nestor uncovered to get rid of King Midas.

rect, reg

king

King for a Day

What laws would you make if you were king for a day? Use your knowledge of *rect/reg* words to write interesting rules.

1. What kind of regalia would you order for the teachers in your kingdom?

   _____

   _____

2. What regimen would you plan for young knights-to-be?

   _____

   _____

3. How would you honor the rectitude of citizens in your kingdom?

   _____

   _____

4. How would you prevent the threat of regicide?

   _____

   _____

5. What regulations would you make regarding the legal age for chariot-driving?

   _____

   _____

6. How would your subjects be required to act toward the regal pets?

   _____

   _____

7. About what problems would you order the rectors of the country to speak?

   _____

   _____

8. When would all citizens be required to hold their arms erect?

   _____

   _____

9. What law would cause people to call you "The Rectangular Ruler"?

   _____

   _____

10. What would be the official motto of your regime?

    _____

    _____

One-Track Mind

People who concentrate on one thing at a time usually produce quality work. Clear out your mental clutter to focus on these words with a *mono/uni* root, meaning "one." For each word, write the letter of the matching definition. Check your answers with a dictionary.

 a. having one spouse
 b. an eyeglass for one eye
 c. religious house where one goes to be alone, away from the world
 d. control of sales by one person or company
 e. having one sound or tone
 f. one single, large stone or monument
 g. fear of being alone
 h. sung with one voice
 i. one of a kind
 j. act of combining separate items into one

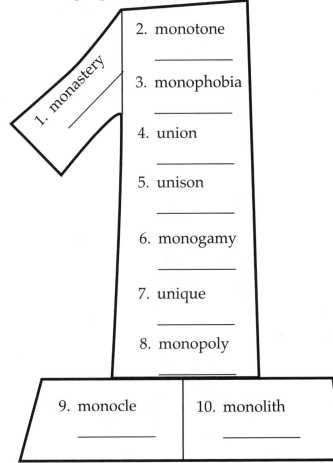

1. monastery _____
2. monotone _____
3. monophobia _____
4. union _____
5. unison _____
6. monogamy _____
7. unique _____
8. monopoly _____
9. monocle _____
10. monolith _____

Picture this! Have some fun with the "look" of these vocabulary words. Add small details to the letter shapes so that the words themselves make a picture of their definitions.

mono⬧ith   mon◉cle

As the Stomach Churns

"As the Stomach Churns" is one of the most popular daytime dramas on television. Read the account below and fill in the missing *mono/uni* words.

The actor playing a wealthy old English duke adjusted his (1)_____ and peered at the script. "One wife? Preposterous! No one believes in (2)_____ on daytime TV. My character might as well go live in a (3)_____!"

The director patted the Duke's face slathered with a (4)_____ assortment of creams and lotions to hide aging. "Now, Sir Charles, you've had a (5)_____ on multiple marriages on this program for years. You've been a (6)_____ to wild living for as long as we've been on the air. It's time your character reformed and settled down to a (7)_____ with one good woman—for life!"

The Duke sighed and began speaking in an exaggerated (8)_____ voice. "Yes—master—your—wish—is—my—com . . ."

Just then, a trio of beautiful young starlets pranced by. "Hello, Charles!" they chorused in (9)_____.

The old actor sprang back to life. "You'll just have to rewrite the script, boss!" he called back as he chased after the girls. "I'm an incurable (10)_____."

One of a Kind?

uni, mono
1
one

Scholars believe that the unicorn was nothing more than the daydream of someone who had heard a traveler's tale about the very real rhinoceros. What a disappointing way to end all those stories about knights and fair damsels and unicorns!

But there are plenty of other things in the world that are unique—like the words below. Use *mono-* or *uni-* to complete each one. Then write the correct number beside each definition.

1. _____ -form
2. _____ -arch
3. _____ -syllabic
4. _____ -verse
5. _____ -ania
6. _____ -gram
7. _____ -corn
8. _____ -theism
9. _____ -logue
10. _____ -chromatic

a. believing in one god
b. lengthy speech given by one person
c. mythical creature with one horn
d. one ruler, king
e. all created things turned into one thing
f. using words of one syllable
g. restricted to one idea
h. consisting of one color
i. single letter or combination of letters to stand for a name
j. having one form

Tell Me Why-O-Why? Refer to your list of all 20 *mono/uni* words to answer these why questions.

A. Why did the British explorer inspect the monolith so carefully with his monocle?

_____

B. Why did the music company have a monopoly on recordings that featured monotone unison singing? _____

_____

C. Why were only monosyllabic words permitted within the walls of the monastery?

_____

D. Why did the bride give her husband a monologue on monogamy? _____

_____

E. Why did the monarch change the monochromatic monograms on all his soldiers' uniforms? _____

_____

Twice as Nice

Double your pleasure, double your fun with these vocabulary words that all mean "two" of something. Find and circle words with the roots *bi* and *du* in the grid below. Then write the number for each word beside the matching definition. Check your answers with a dictionary.

1. bicuspid
2. bicep
3. bifocal
4. dialogue
5. duel

6. biped
7. bicentennial
8. bilingual
9. duet
10. duplicity

```
            J D U E L
          B I L I N G U A L
                    E B P
                    U I E
                    G F C
                    O O I
                    Y C B
              J T A A
              R I E I L
          S B C O U D
          S I N K D
        A L P M Y
      E P Y E K
    C U V W D I A L O G U E
    D B O X B I C U S P I D
    B I C E N T E N N I A L
```

_____ a. a conversation between two people

_____ b. double-dealing, trickery

_____ c. a two-footed creature

_____ d. speaking two languages

_____ e. music for two performers

_____ f. a two-pointed tooth located in the side of the jaw

_____ g. occurring every two hundred years

_____ h. combat between two people or armies

_____ i. having two centers of vision

_____ j. a muscle having two origins

Double Trouble

All the bumper stickers below feature *bi/du* words. For each one, select the person most likely to have the sticker on his or her car; then explain why.

a. a dental patient
b. a peace-lover
c. an eyeglass wearer
d. a fencing team member
e. a choir director
f. a good conversationalist
g. a bicep builder
h. a mother or father
i. a bicentennial celebration planner
j. a foreign language teacher

	WHO?	WHY?
1. Just Duet!	_____	_____
2. Avoid duplicity Seek simplicity.	_____	_____
3. Small biped on board	_____	_____
4. I brake for bilinguals	_____	_____
5. Dueling Dad	_____	_____
6. My bicuspids and my money go to Dr. Booth	_____	_____
7. Want some dialogue? Dial 1-800-TALK.	_____	_____
8. Marvelous Maysville 200 Years Young!	_____	_____
9. Bifocal yokel and proud of it!	_____	_____
10. Muscles matter!	_____	_____

bi , du

2

two

Show and Tell

For each situation below, draw a cartoon and write appropriate words.

1. Show a biped with bifocals. Tell what he says as he stares at his feet.

2. Show a bilingual dialogue. Tell some of the conversation.

3. Show a dentist dueling with a stubborn bicuspid. Tell what he says when he succeeds.

4. Show a bicentennial birthday cake. Tell what the recipient says.

5. Show a pet duet. Tell what the neighbors say.

6. Show a guy's duplicity in taking two dates to a dance. Tell what the girls say.

7. Show a baby with great biceps. Tell what the pediatrician says.

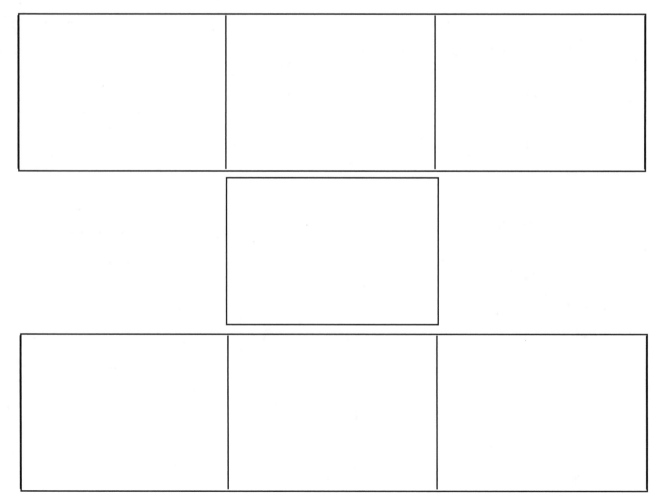

Paint By Number

It's easy to make a masterpiece—if you go by the numbers! All the vocabulary words below contain roots that indicate a number value:

tri = 3   *quad* = 4   *quint/pent* = 5   *dec* = 10   *cent* = 100

For each word, write the letter of the matching definition. Check your answers with a dictionary.

a. a polygon having five sides
b. a period of 100 years
c. a series of three books or plays
d. a ten-footed creature, such as a crab or shrimp
e. a three-pronged spear
f. an insect with many legs
g. a forty-year-old
h. the Ten Commandments
i. one of five babies born at one birth
j. a four-footed creature

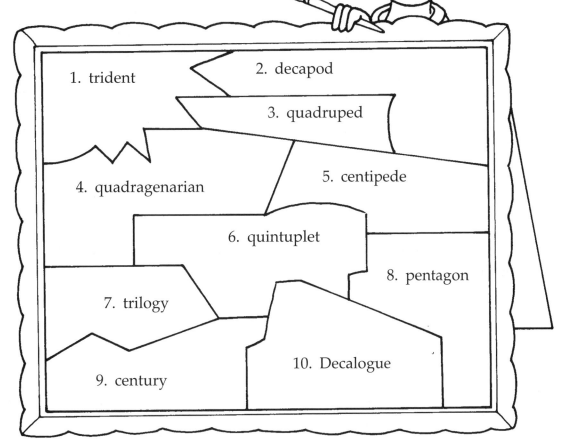

1. trident
2. decapod
3. quadruped
4. quadragenarian
5. centipede
6. quintuplet
7. trilogy
8. pentagon
9. century
10. Decalogue

Now add color to this work of art:

3 = red   4 = blue   5 = green   10 = yellow   100 = orange

The Scoop Shoppe

Everyone loves ice cream! At the Scoop Shoppe, there's a taste treat for every appetite. Use your knowledge of vocabulary to pair each flavor with the matching customer.

_____ 1. Curried Crab Crunch

_____ 2. Slow-Melt Marshmallow

_____ 3. Angel-Touch Ambrosia

_____ 4. Five-Star Fudge

_____ 5. Chocolate Raspberry
Chocolate Strawberry
Chocolate Huckleberry

_____ 6. Deviled Ham Custard

_____ 7. Very Low-Fat Vanilla

_____ 8. Rainbow Sherbet
a blend of 5 flavors

_____ 9. Frozen T-Bone Treat

_____ 10. Centipede Sundae

a. designed for high-ranking Pentagon officials
b. a trilogy of delicious flavors
c. the one to buy when you have quintuplets to satisfy
d. you'll go buggy over this creamy confection topped with hundreds of little legs
e. a flavor reserved for those who have kept every law of the Decalogue
f. for decapod-lovers
g. now you can treat your quadruped, too
h. for trident-toters only
i. for quadragenarians watching middle-age spread
j. it lasts for a century

How many different flavors of ice cream does The Scoop Shoppe actually sell? Jot down the number from the meaning of each vocabulary word used above. Add to find the answer.

_____ flavors

Your Lucky Number

Knowing number roots is just like having a lucky number—you discover you have the key to hundreds of interesting words. Use root knowledge to answer each question below with a number. Then add your totals. If the sum is 372, you've hit the jackpot!

1. How many sheets of paper do you have with triplicate copies? _____
2. How old is a centenarian? _____
3. How many points does the star known as a pentagram have? _____
4. How many syllables does a decasyllabic word contain? _____
5. The centigrade scale for measuring temperature is based on how many degrees?

   _____
6. If you trisect a pie, how many boys can you feed? _____
7. How many singers does it take to make up a quartet? _____
8. The ancient Greeks divided the universe into basic categories. The quintessence was the last. How many categories were there? _____ (Today the word means "the most concentrated form of a thing." Example: The ballerina was the quintessence of grace.)
9. Which month was December on the early Roman calendar? _____
10. How many angles does a quadrilateral have? _____
11. A punishment often handed out in ancient Roman times was to decimate the male population. Soldiers executed one man out of every _____.
12. How many aspects does a trinity contain? _____
13. A Roman centurion was in command of how many soldiers? _____
14. How many sides does a decagon have? _____
15. How many books make up the part of the Bible known as the Pentateuch? _____

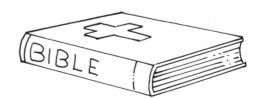

spec, spic

look

Through the Looking Glass

Look into Alice's mirror for vocabulary words that share the root *spec* or *spic,* meaning "to look." Beside each mirror word, write the correct spelling; then match it with the correct definition. Check your answers with a dictionary.

_____ 1. etaluceps = _____

_____ 2. retceps = _____

_____ 3. murtceps = _____

_____ 4. nemiceps = _____

_____ 5. suoicipsus = _____

_____ 6. rotatceps = _____

_____ 7. elcatceps = _____

_____ 8. muluceps = _____

_____ 9. evitcepsorter = _____

_____ 10. suoucipsnoc = _____

a. a noteworthy sight to see
b. an onlooker
c. very easy to see, noticeable
d. a ghostly vision
e. colors one sees when light is broken into waves, as with a prism
f. mirror used to look into body cavities
g. to see a mental picture
h. a sample that looks like all those of the same group
i. a look back at the past
j. distrustful-looking

Here's how to do some mirror-writing on your own. First, use thin paper and write an original sentence of seven words or more for each vocabulary word. When you have finished, flip the paper over and place another thin sheet on top. Go over the backwards letters that show through. Then give your mirror-writing to a friend to decode.

A Closer Look

spec, spic

look

Match each cartoon with the correct vocabulary word. Write the words on the lines.

speculate

suspicious

spectacle

specter

specimen

speculum

conspicuous

spectators

retrospective

spectrum

spec, spic

look

Match these tools and devices used by ghostbusters with the correct explanations.

_____ 1. a retrospective speculum
_____ 2. a suspicious specimen
_____ 3. spectrum spray
_____ 4. a speculation sta
_____ 5. a spectacle meter
_____ 6. the conspicuous spring

a. a paint containing all seven colors, for making invisible spirits visible
b. a device for looking into a ghostly body to see events that occurred in it in the past
c. a hand-held device that observes all details during a ghostly encounter and prints out a written analysis afterwards
d. tells just how noteworthy a ghostly appearance is; helps you measure and compare with other appearances
e. a very noticeable coil that attracts and traps ghosts
f. a sample of blue-white membrane that indicates what ghost flesh is like

Now create your own customized specter. Dress your ghost in retrospective clothing. Show suspicious red stains on the hands. Color the ghost every shade of the spectrum to make it conspicuous. Show spectators' reaction to your ghost.

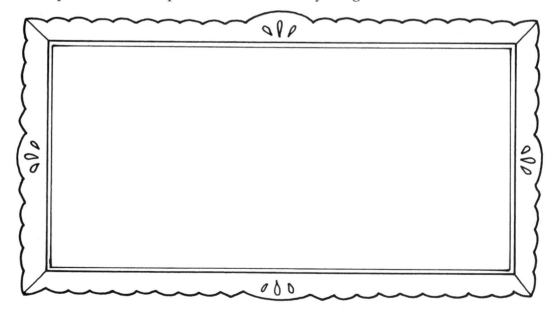

Top Secret

Which is more powerful, the pen or the sword? When you consider the number of words that include the idea of writing, the pen wins by an ink barrel! All of the words below share the root *graph* or *gram*, "to write." Match each word with the correct definition. Use a dictionary to check your answers.

a. story of one's own life written by oneself
b. a person's own handwriting
c. the tracing (writing) made by a heart monitor
d. a saying written on a building or statue
e. rules for using the written word
f. anything written, drawn, or printed
g. the study of handwriting and what it reveals about a person
h. writing words with correct spelling
i. a division of a written work
j. a story of a person's life

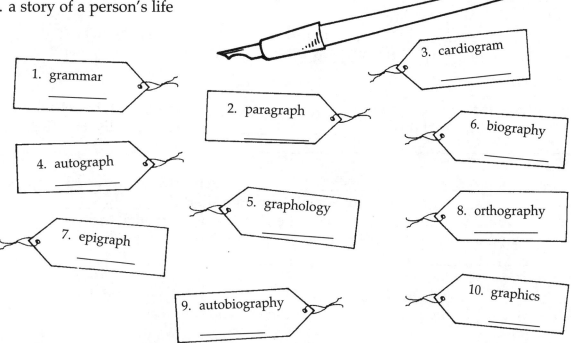

Now send some secret messages. For each vocabulary term, create a sentence of seven words or more. Dip a toothpick (or other pointed tip) in lemon juice and write each sentence on a strip of notebook paper. When the juice dries, your writing will be almost invisible! To reveal the message, hold the strip of paper over a glowing light bulb. The heat will make your words turn brown. (Note: Do not wait too long to "develop" the invisible writing. After several hours, paper absorbs the acid of the lemon juice so that it will not turn dark when exposed to heat.)

Last Will and Testament

It is never too early to get your affairs in order. The will below contains two types of blanks. In the numbered blanks, write the correct vocabulary words. In the starred blanks, add personalized information to make this will your very own!

I, *_____, being of sound mind and body, record these instructions as my last will and testament before I depart this life.

To *_____, *_____, and *_____, I leave (1) _____ copies of my (2)_____ so you will never forget one moment of my fascinating life.

To my teachers, *_____ and *_____ at *_____ School, I leave free (3)_____ at *_____ Hospital. Having me has been such an electrifying experience, you deserve to get your hearts checked.

To *_____, I leave my favorite pen. Now all those personal notes you pass in class can be written in style, worthy of examination by students of (4)_____.

With gratitude and appreciation to *_____ School, I hereby set aside funds for the engraving of this (5)_____ on the side of the building: *_____ .

To *_____ and *_____, who always corrected my (6)_____ and split my long papers into short (7)_____, I leaves two dozen reports, so you can have the pleasure of making all them little red squiggles which shows everything I never wanted to know about (6)_____ and (7) _____.

To *_____, who drew great (8)_____ on the bathroom walls, I leave a bottle of cleaner and a scrub brush so you can clean up your act!

To *_____, who always copied ansers (usially rong) from my spelling tests, I leave an (9)_____ book and a dikshunairy.

To *_____ and *_____, I leave my (10)_____ of great world leaders. It never hurts to read about success. Who knows? Some of it just might rub off on you!

Signed: *_____

With Pen in Hand

There are books written for every interest—all you have to do is look!
Match each title below with the correct description.

_____ 1. Graphology in Police work

_____ 2. Grammar in the Slammer

_____ 3. Painless Paragraphing

_____ 4. I Kant Spel Gud

_____ 5. Earnest Epigraphs

_____ 6. ME! ME! ME!

_____ 7. Heartbeats & Hammers

_____ 8. The Graphic Grandchild

_____ 9. Beastly Biographies

_____ 10. Autograph of a Great Man

a. the autobiography of a self-centered snob

b. an easy-to-use guide to dividing your written words into sensible units

c. raise your children's children to be gifted in drawing and printing

d. for detectives cracking down on check forgery

e. the biography of John Hancock

f. a traveler's guide to the serious slogans written on America's buildings

g. a study of the written word as used in America's prisons

h. confessions of an orthography drop-out

i. the cardiograms of carpenters and what we learn from them

j. true-life tales of real animals

carn, corp **body**

Mr. Tee

Two Latin roots, *carn* and *corp*, are so close in meaning, it is fun to study them together. *Carn* means "flesh" or "red meat"; *orp* refers to the "whole body." Listed below are words that stem from these two roots. Write the letter of each word on the matching definition T-shirt.

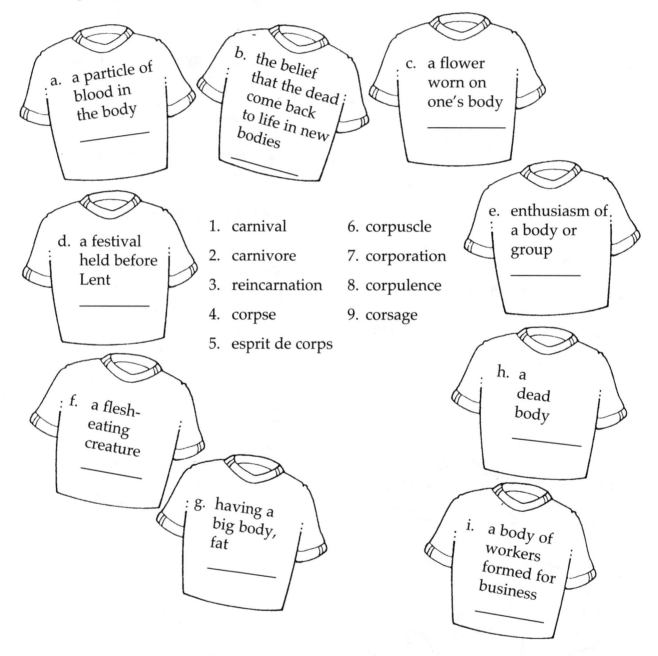

a. a particle of blood in the body

b. the belief that the dead come back to life in new bodies

c. a flower worn on one's body

d. a festival held before Lent

e. enthusiasm of a body or group

f. a flesh-eating creature

g. having a big body, fat

h. a dead body

i. a body of workers formed for business

1. carnival
2. carnivore
3. reincarnation
4. corpse
5. esprit de corps
6. corpuscle
7. corporation
8. corpulence
9. corsage

Turn those T-shirts into helpful flashcards. Cut them out and write the correct vocabulary word on the back of each. Flip through the shirts two times every day this week for painless vocabulary mastery.

Meet Me at the Mall

carn, corp
body

It's shopping time! Which stores should we visit? Write the letter of each description below the matching store.

a. a store that specializes in dinosaur items: toys, T-shirts, posters, models
b. a book store featuring accounts of people who died and came back to life in different bodies
c. for all your cheerleading squad's needs
d. high-quality dissection specimens for scientists, teachers, and students—from earthworms to pigs
e. flattering clothing to make every size body appear slimmer
f. flowers-to-go for weddings, proms, and special occasions
g. interesting imports from a body of Caribbean craftsmen
h. a candy store specializing in pre-Lenten sweets
i. a gym where you can lift weights and give blood to the Red Cross in one convenient stop!

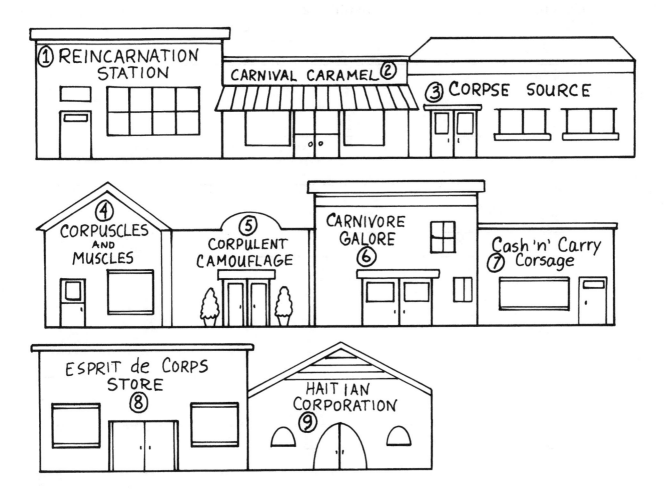

carn, corp
body

Simon Says

Follow the directions regarding your flesh and body:

1. SIMON SAYS: Act like a carnivore spotting his next meal.
2. SIMON SAYS: Create some esprit de corps! Lead the class in a cheer about vocabulary.
3. SIMON SAYS: Pin an invisible corsage on every female in the room.
4. SIMON SAYS: Enlist two friends and be corpuscles attacking a virus.
5. SIMON SAYS: Demonstrate an exercise that will reduce corpulence.
6. SIMON SAYS: Enlist a group and pantomime the work of a corporation. Ask the class to guess what the corporation is.
7. SIMON SAYS: Show how it feels to be reincarnated as a bird.
8. SIMON SAYS: Enlist friends and pantomime a carnival ride. Ask the class to guess what the ride is.
9. SIMON SAYS: Do mock battle with friends until there is nothing left but carnage.
10. SIMON SAYS: Identify a corpse in a police morgue.

Now write five SIMON SAYS clues of your own, using body vocabulary. Perform them for your classmates. Can they correctly identify each word?

1. _____
   _____
   _____

2. _____
   _____
   _____

3. _____
   _____
   _____

4. _____
   _____
   _____

5. _____
   _____
   _____

curr, curs, cours

run

In the Running

When you know vocabulary roots, you can really make tracks! The ancient Latin word for "running" or "flowing" appears in modern English words as *curr*, *curs*, or *cours*. Match these definitions with the words on the running shoe below. Check your answers with a dictionary.

a. a running flow, as of water or electricity
b. the entire run of courses offered to a student
c. a runner, messenger
d. flowing writing
e. forerunner
f. one who runs from the law, a pirate
g. a swift-running horse
h. quick, as a glance
i. a long-running speech
j. a long, running hallway

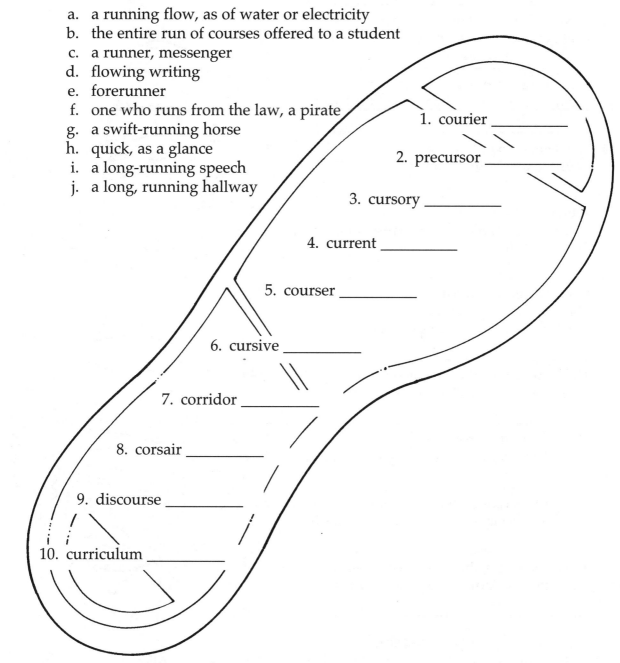

1. courier _____
2. precursor _____
3. cursory _____
4. current _____
5. courser _____
6. cursive _____
7. corridor _____
8. corsair _____
9. discourse _____
10. curriculum _____

Now trace your own running shoe and cut out ten footprints. On each one write an original sentence of seven words or more. Post your prints in paths that lead everywhere—up your locker, into the corner, even across the ceiling!

Rhymes on the Run

Who is it? Match these vocabulary clues with the names appearing in the Personality Bank.

1. With Silver, his courser, and Tonto, his friend,
   He kept the West safe from end to end.

   _____

2. "Hang one for land or two for sea,
   And I on the opposite shore will be," this courier said.

   _____

3. One cursory glance, and she felt terrific.
   She had led the first white men to the Pacific!

   _____

4. This famous '50s TV horse
   Loved to discourse, of course.

   _____

5. A bit of cursive sealed his fate
   And spoiled his plan to open West Point's gate
   To the British.

   _____

6. His curriculum covered it all:
   Makeup and juggling balls,
   Tumbling tricks and practicing falls.

   _____

7. The current carried them down the mighty Mississip—
   For these two lads, a life-changing trip.

   _____ _____

8. "Drink me," the label said.
   Then she hit the corridor ceiling with her head.

   _____

9. Precursor of cartoon characters down through the years,
   He is known for his squeaky voice and his big ears.

   _____

10. To frighten folks, this infamous corsair
    Liked to stick burning matches in his hair.

    _____

PERSONALITY BANK

Paul Revere	Mr. Ed	Alice
Blackbeard	Sacagawea	Emmett Kelly
Lone Ranger	Benedict Arnold	Mickey Mouse
	Tom Sawyer	Huckleberry Finn

Mixed Messages

In 1861 the Pony Express was the fastest way to send a message across the United States. A copy of Abraham Lincoln's first speech to Congress arrived in California only 7 days and 17 hours after he gave it! Express riders worked day and night, riding through rough weather and dangerous territory. The service was a model of dedication and efficiency.

But in *this* Pony Express office, the mail is a mess! Somehow, the messages have become tangled. Read each sentence and decide whether the vocabulary word is used correctly. If it is, place a check on the line. On the back of this sheet, rewrite any incorrect sentences to show how to use the vocabulary word properly.

_____ 1. Dear Students: Cursory language is inappropriate in public places and punishable at this school.

_____ 2. Dear Martha: To shelter all our cows from the bitter weather, I have added a tiny corridor at the back of the cabin.

_____ 3. Dear Jimmy: Did you know that the Pony Express was the precursor of today's overnight mail service?

_____ 4. Dear Mr. Ebenezer: Enclosed is the home study guide to gold-mining you requested. If the material does not prove to be helpful, you may discourse it.

_____ 5. Dear Mother: Mounted on his famous courser Traveler, General Robert E. Lee was a familiar and encouraging sight to all of us soldiers.

_____ 6. Dear Sirs: Please send your reply immediately by corsair.

_____ 7. Dear Clementine: I am so excited about the Officers' Ball. I put on my gown and practiced making cursives all night!

_____ 8. Dear Father: Old Blue won a ribbon at the Exhibition! I curriculumed him for hours before the judging began.

_____ 9. Dearest Sister: How can I ever thank you for the current of understanding that flows between us?

_____ 10. Dear Mrs. Smith: The courier will arrive promptly at 9 a.m. Please have your financial records available for his in-depth examination.

The Golden Rule

Does following the Golden Rule make you an angel? No, but it certainly does not hurt your chances! All the words listed below share the Greek root *arch*, with the common meaning of "ruler" or "chief." For each definition on the angel's wings, write the correct vocabulary word. Check your answers with a dictionary.

a. archangel
b. archenemy
c. archrival
d. anarchy
e. monarch

f. hierarchy
g. archipelago
h. architect
i. archive
j. archetype

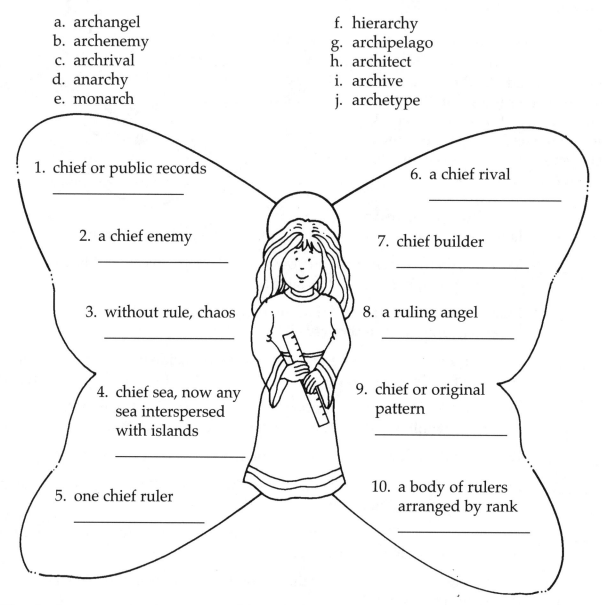

1. chief or public records
   _____

2. a chief enemy
   _____

3. without rule, chaos
   _____

4. chief sea, now any sea interspersed with islands
   _____

5. one chief ruler
   _____

6. a chief rival
   _____

7. chief builder
   _____

8. a ruling angel
   _____

9. chief or original pattern
   _____

10. a body of rulers arranged by rank
    _____

What is the connection between each vocabulary word and following the rules? Write a sentence for each. (Example: A monarch makes the rules that his/her subjects must follow.)

Now for some fun! Use the shape above as a pattern to cut an angel out of lightweight tissue paper. Fold down the middle lengthwise. Next, take a drinking straw and blow your angel into the air. How long can you keep it flying?

On Cloud Nine

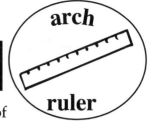

arch

ruler

Fill in the blanks with vocabulary words to read a story that is "out of this world"!

It was choir practice hour on Cloud Nine, and Eleazar, the littlest cherub of all, giggled as his best friend and (1)_____, Hector, hit a sour note.

Michael, (2) _____and choir director, looked up. "Hector, have you been practicing? I will send you down to work on the most remote (3)_____ on that miserable planet Earth if you are not careful. You and Eleazar step forward. Let's hear you two on the new songs."

Eleazar gulped and joined Hector down front. With quivering voices, they began singing hymns that celebrated their king, the great (4)_____ of Heaven.

"(5)_____ of the Universe, who
designed and built the stars and the planets . . .
"You are the Head of the Heavenly (6)_____
All others bow before you. . .
"You alone are praised in all the (7)_____
kept by all the prophets. . .
"Only you could defeat the (8)_____ Satan,
the author of (9)_____ and confusion. . .

The two little angels suddenly stopped in mid-chorus. The King Himself stood before them. The entire choir bowed low.

"Come, young ones," the King's majestic voice boomed. "Come and see. I have just made the (10)_____ for the whole human race. I think I will call them Adam and Eve. . . ."

What happens next? Write a continuation of this story using all ten vocabulary words.

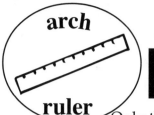

arch
ruler

History/Mysteries

Only the heavens have witnessed all of mankind's history. Solve these history/mysteries. You may use any reference books you wish to locate the answers.

1. Who was the last ruling monarch of Hawaii? _____

2. Name and locate two archipelagos. _____

3. Who was the architect of the Taj Mahal? _____

4. What documents are on display at the National Archives in Washington, D. C.? ___
   _____

5. Name two famous archangels. _____

6. Who is Popeye's archrival for Olive Oyl's affection? _____

7. Name the twenty-fifth president of the United States who was assassinated by an anarchist.
   _____

8. What was the archetype for today's mass-produced automobile? _____

9. Name the two families in Shakespeare's drama *Romeo and Juliet,* who were age-old archenemies. _____

10. List the hierarchy of titles from lowest to highest that make up the British nobility.
    _____

Now write three history/mysteries of your own, using *arch* vocabulary. See if your classmates can locate the correct answers! _____

By the Book

Include the root words *cycl* and *orb* in your vocabulary circle, for they both share the idea of "roundness." Modern English words use that meaning in surprising ways. For example, what does the set of encyclopedias below have to do with a circle? Let's find out!

Beside each vocabulary word write the letter of the matching definition. Check your answers with a dictionary.

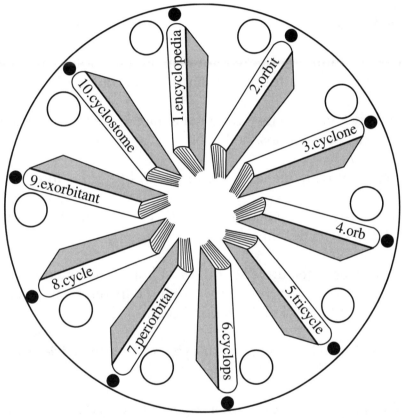

a. three-wheeled vehicle
b. a circular windstorm
c. a complete circle of events that occurs repeatedly
d. a giant with one round eye in the middle of this forehead
e. a summary of the entire circle of knowledge

f. an eel-like fish with a round sucking mouth
g. a round body; the sun, the eye
h. going beyond the normal circle; excessive
i. a circular path
j. area around the eye

Now cut out the wheel and punch a hole by each book. Poke a pencil point in the hole and flip the wheel over to the back side. Write the definition that corresponds to the vocabulary word on the front beside the hole. Do this for all ten words. Now you have your own circle of knowledge and a quick easy way to review *cycl* and *orb* vocabulary.

cycl , orb

roundness

The Hall of the Horrid

We are visiting the Hall of the Horrid, a wax museum featuring famous underworld figures. Use the vocabulary clues to match each description with the correct name.

a. Cyclone Ione
b. Sunburn Sam
c. Cyclops
d. Pop Sickle
e. Terrible Trixie

f. Encyclopedia Sid
g. The Creep from the Deep
h. Raccoon June
i. Jewel
j. Orson Orbit

_____ 1. A matronly murderer decked out in exorbitant clothes and jewelry. Her favorite punishment for her prisoners? Pounding-by-Pearls.

_____ 2. An undersea villain. His weapon of choice is the Super Sucker, an enormous cyclostome that suctions the life out of his victims.

_____ 3. A hairy giant with one large eye in the middle of his forehead.

_____ 4. The scholar-crook. He drives his victims mad by reciting entire volumes of knowledge as he ties them up.

_____ 5. The old-timer of the underworld. Most known for the cycle he repeats at every crime scene: carefully unwrapping a frozen treat, licking it slowly, then shoving the stick in his victim's ear.

_____ 6. A criminal with burning orbs for eyes, so intense he fries everyone at whom he stares.

_____ 7. A child monster who rides on a supersonic tricycle equipped with toys that are actually dangerous.

_____ 8. Easily recognized by the deep purple periorbital makeup she wears. Rummages through trash cans in the dark.

_____ 9. A female monster who travels in a whirlwind, picking up anything in her path and hurling it at her enemies.

_____ 10. Often seen in the company of Cyclone Ione. No matter where he goes, he walks in a circular path, throwing the police off his trail with ease.

Pick three members of the Hall of the Horrid to illustrate.

Twister

We are off to Oz with Dorothy—along with lots of other stuff! Read the vocabulary clues. Draw and label the objects caught up by the twister below.

1. a three-wheeled recreational vehicle

2. an exorbitant diamond necklace

3. a summary of the entire circle of plumbing knowledge

4. a fly orbiting a cheeseburger

5. protective periorbital spectacles

6. a cyclostome looking for lunch

7. a Cyclops mask

8. a Cyclone Zone warning sign

9. a laundry product used in the rinse cycle

10. a box of glass orbs

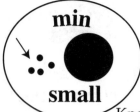
min

small

Small Change

Knowing vocabulary roots is like having coins in the bank. They are there whenever you need them! For each definition on the coins below, write the letter of the correct word using *min*, meaning "small." Check your answers with a dictionary.

1. very small

_____

2. smaller, underage

_____

3. a dance marked by small steps

_____

4. to cut into very small pieces

_____

5. the least amount possible

_____

6. less

_____

a. mince   f. minute
b. miniature   g. minister
c. minimum   h. minus
d. minuet   i. minor
e. minuscule   j. minstrel

7. marked by attention to small details

_____

8. a lesser person who serves by entertaining

_____

9. a small copy

_____

10. a lesser person who serves by helping

_____

Big bank accounts and large vocabularies are not built overnight—it takes time and effort for both. On the back of your paper, use each vocabulary word in a paragraph to finish this story:

"For years, I had been saving minuscule amounts of money, tucking away fifty cents here, two dollars there. But the day I walked by Sawyer's Department Store window and saw . . . ."

It's a Small World

min

small

Use *min* vocabulary to fill in the blanks in the newspaper article below. Find out the real story behind this famous literary character!

Yesterday in Small Claims Court, a (1)_____, Tom T. Piperson, was found guilty of stealing one of Reverend Trever's pigs. The (2)_____, a keen observer of (3)_____ details, noticed he was (4)_____ one swine when he took a bucket of (5)_____ marshmallows out to the pig pen.

The evidence that clinched Tom's guilt was the (6)_____ amount of barbecued pork clinging to his lips.

The boy, sentenced to the (7)_____ punishment of 30 licks with a (8)_____ matchstick, sobbed on his lawyer's shoulder. But outside the courtroom, (9)_____ danced a (10)_____ celebrating their new jingle now being sung all over town:

> "Tom, Tom T. Piperson stole a pig and away did run.
> The pig was eat, Tom was beat,
> And Tom went crying down the street!"

Now take a minute and solve these minute riddles by placing

the number on the blank beside the correct definition.

_____	a.	The modern-day version of an old-fashioned dance
_____	b.	A miniature mess
_____	c.	The king of budget deficits
_____	d.	The instrument played by Tom Thumb
_____	e.	An underage complainer
_____	f.	An evil public servant
_____	g.	The minimum Thanksgiving meal
_____	h.	A tiny amount of sewing thread
_____	i.	A boastful minstrel
_____	j.	The owner of a knife company

1. a minor whiner
2. the Minus Highness
3. a sinister minister
4. a jet-set minuet
5. a small but sloppy copy
6. a minute flute
7. the Prince of Mince
8. the vainer entertainer
9. a minuscule spool
10. a least feast

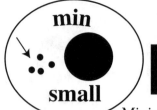

min

small

Fore!

Miniature golf can certainly enlarge your vocabulary! To play the game below, you will need a stack of cards, one vocabulary word and its meaning to a card, two small game markers, and a penny.

Place the cards face down on the desk. To get to move, you must give your partner the correct definition for the word card he/she draws from the stack. If you are right, flip the penny. Heads, you move ahead three spaces; tails, you move one. Then obey the commands on the gameboard. First to the finish line is a golf pro and a vocabulary whiz!

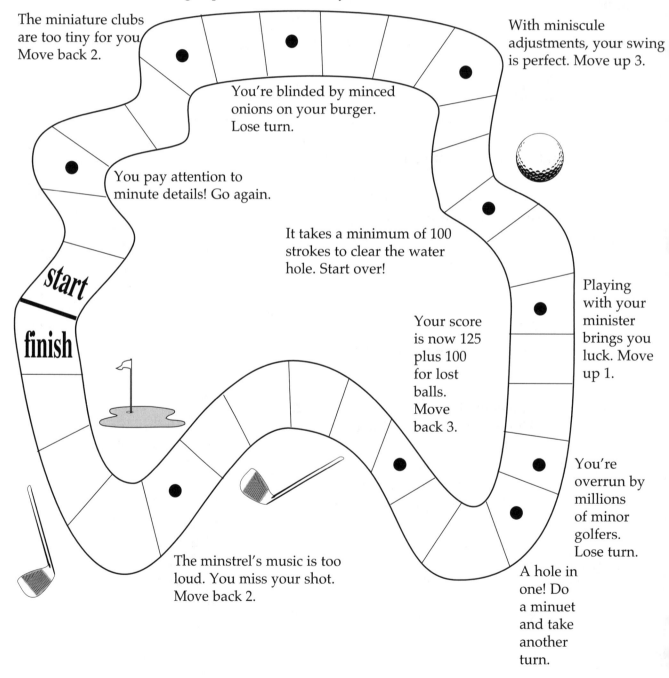

The miniature clubs are too tiny for you. Move back 2.

With miniscule adjustments, your swing is perfect. Move up 3.

You're blinded by minced onions on your burger. Lose turn.

You pay attention to minute details! Go again.

It takes a minimum of 100 strokes to clear the water hole. Start over!

start

finish

Playing with your minister brings you luck. Move up 1.

Your score is now 125 plus 100 for lost balls. Move back 3.

You're overrun by millions of minor golfers. Lose turn.

The minstrel's music is too loud. You miss your shot. Move back 2.

A hole in one! Do a minuet and take another turn.

Do You Hear What I Hear?

phon

sound

What ever would we do without our ears? They allow us to hear pleasant music, warning sirens, the singing of birds, and the crash of the surf. They also help us keep our balance!

All of the words in the ear maze below come from the root word *phon*, meaning "sound." For each definition, write the number of the matching word in the blank. Check your answers with a dictionary.

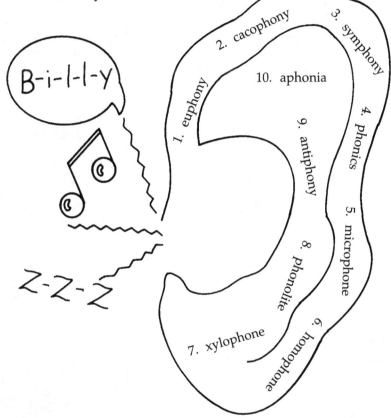

_____ a. an instrument of wooden bars that makes a ringing sound when struck

_____ b. the science of sounds, used as a method of teaching reading

_____ c. beautiful sounds

_____ d. a series of musical answers sung back and forth between groups

_____ e. harsh sounds

_____ f. an instrument for intensifying small sounds

_____ g. loss of voice due to paralysis of the vocal cords

_____ h. instrumental piece in which musicians play together

_____ i. a letter or word expressing the same sound as another

_____ j. type of volcanic rock that makes a ringing sound when struck

Sounds Phishy to Me!

Match each cartoon with the correct vocabulary word. Write the words on the lines.

1. _____

2. _____

3. _____

4. _____

phonics
antiphony
phonolite
aphonia
euphony
symphony
microphone
homophone
xylophone
cacophony

5. _____

6. _____

7. _____

8. _____

9. _____

10. _____

Telephony Baloney

phon
sound

The telephone is a marvelous invention—until it falls into the hands of a persistent salesperson! Eavesdrop on these telemarketing sales calls and fill in the missing vocabulary words.

1. "Hello, Ma'am. Are your children so noisy at the dinner table, you can't hear yourself speak? Then let me tell you about a wonderful new product, The Mother's _____."

2. "When you become a member of the _____ Hotline, help with words that sound alike is only a phone call away."

3. "Now, Mr. Sullivan, I'm sure you will be happy to learn that even the most nonmusical member of your family can learn to play the Hi/Lo _____."

4. "Good evening, sir. Do you respect rocks? Do minerals mesmerize you? Now you can begin a stunning rock collection with your very own specimen of _____, the musical mineral."

5. "Sir, you have been preapproved for a 60-day trial supply of_____ -Phree. Now you no longer have to worry about losing your voice at just the wrong moment."

6. "Madam, I am calling on behalf of the music-lovers of your community. Could I interest you in season tickets to the _____?"

7. "Experience the beautiful sounds of French fountains, German brooks, and Austrian meadows. Mrs. Smith, may we send this marvelous CD, European _____, to you today for your listening pleasure?"

8. "Mr. Jones, we are conducting a telephone survey in your area today. What percentage of your normal household noise would you consider to be _____? Then we have an earplug product that will block out all that unpleasantness."

9. "Hi, this is Fannie with Over-40 _____. May I speak with an adult non-reader, please?"

10. "Mrs. Brown, I am a school teacher, the same as you. If your students are like mine, they get tired of the typical questions and answers, day in and day out. But I have good news! With our new book, Musical Messages, you can transform your teaching with _____ singing.

anthro, homo
man

Human Beans

The root words *anthro*, *homo*, and *hum* all mean the same thing, "mankind." For each box below, write the letter of the matching definition. Check your answers with a dictionary. Then add details to the human "beans" to illustrate the words.

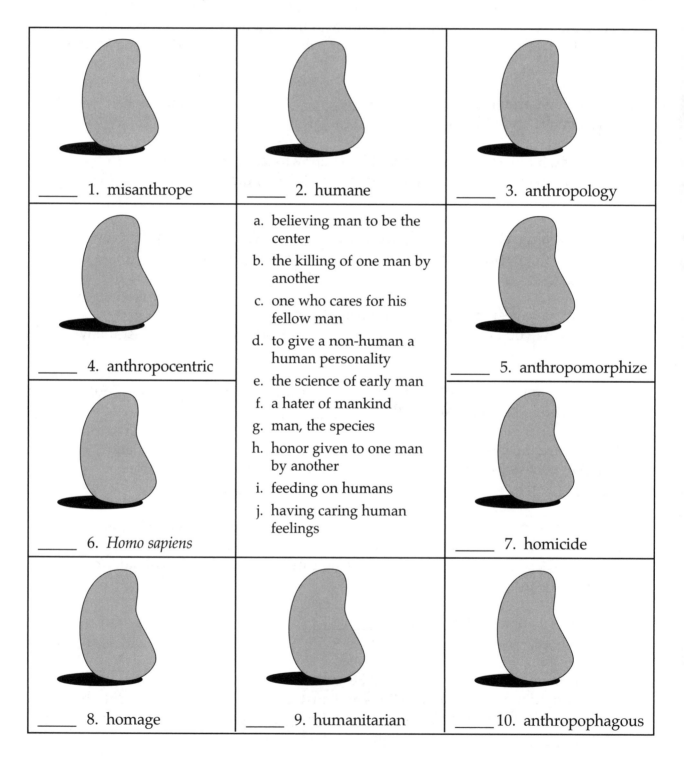

_____ 1. misanthrope

_____ 2. humane

_____ 3. anthropology

_____ 4. anthropocentric

a. believing man to be the center

b. the killing of one man by another

c. one who cares for his fellow man

d. to give a non-human a human personality

e. the science of early man

f. a hater of mankind

g. man, the species

h. honor given to one man by another

i. feeding on humans

j. having caring human feelings

_____ 5. anthropomorphize

_____ 6. *Homo sapiens*

_____ 7. homicide

_____ 8. homage

_____ 9. humanitarian

_____ 10. anthropophagous

A Whale of a Tale

anthro, homo

man

Here is a new twist on an old familiar story. Fill in each blank with the correct vocabulary word.

Way back when the world was young, O Best Beloved, from the time of the earliest (1)_____, the time that addled (2)_____ like to study and study, there lived a man named Jonah.

Now the Master Planner had planned a plan for his man Jonah, and he said, "Yo, Jonah Man, go yonder to sinful city of Nineveh. Be a (3)_____ and warn the people to behave themselves. Otherwise, I will annihilate Nineveh with wholesale (4)_____."

But Jonah, being the miserable (5)_____ that he was, hating the nasties in Nineveh, and paying no (6)_____ whatsoever to the Master Planner, said, "Later, dude." Then he immediately hopped onboard a ship heading in the opposite direction.

So the Master Planner shook the ocean and woke up the waves, and Jonah landed right smack in the middle of the Deep Blue Sea. Now the Deep Blue was swarming with (7)_____ bacteria, those tee-tiny organisms who feast on flabby, flubbery flesh. It was teatime on the sea, and the tiny terrorists were hungry, and our man Jonah, fearing for his life, began to babble and belch.

But from the depths of the Deep Dark rumbled a Deep Dark (8)_____ whale of a voice, "We're s-s-s-so much more (9)_____ than you (10)_____ human beings. You little people have to be at the c-c-center of e-e-everything. Well, h-h-here's the c-c-center of s-s-something n-n-new."

And with that, the whale opened his monstrous mouth.

Poor Jonah! What happens next? Continue the story. Use all 10 vocabulary words.

anthro, homo
man

Human Headlines

Below are the newspaper headlines for some human interest stories. Write the lead sentence for each one. Make certain that you explain the meaning of all vocabulary words included in the headlines. You may use a dictionary for help.

1. Anonymous Anthropologist Apologizes to Apes: "We're Really Not Related" _____

_____

_____

2. Report from Space: Citizens of Saturn Pattern Similar Anthropocentric Sentiments

_____

_____

3. Washington Wise Guys Anthropomorphize Flies Amidst Public Outcries

_____

_____

4. Alaskan Huskies Hostile to Hotheaded *Homo Sapiens* _____

_____

5. Ominous Omelet Homicide Omen of Fowl Play_____

_____

_____

6. Homage to Hominy, Hoecakes, and Homespun_____

_____

_____

7. Humane Campaign to Relieve Brain Pain, Doctors Outlaw Homework and Tests!

_____

_____

8. Foggy about the Anthropophagi? These Folks Forage for Flesh _____

_____

_____

9. Humanitarian Prairie Librarian Marries Merry Millionarian _____

_____

_____

Speak Your Mind!

dict

speak

Nothing reveals our thoughts more clearly than our speech—the terms we choose, our tone, our accents. All the words below include the idea of "speaking," from the Latin root *dict*. Find and circle each word in the search, then write the number beside the matching definition. Check your answers with a dictionary.

1. diction
2. edict
3. contradict
4. dictation
5. indictment

6. dictionary
7. predict
8. verdict
9. dictator
10. dictum

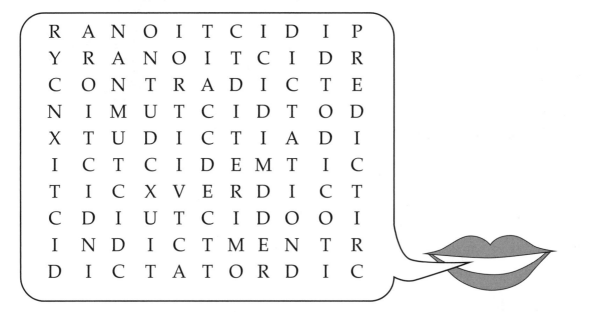

```
R  A  N  O  I  T  C  I  D  I  P
Y  R  A  N  O  I  T  C  I  D  R
C  O  N  T  R  A  D  I  C  T  E
N  I  M  U  T  C  I  D  T  O  D
X  T  U  D  I  C  T  I  A  D  I
I  C  T  C  I  D  E  M  T  I  C
T  I  C  X  V  E  R  D  I  C  T
C  D  I  U  T  C  I  D  O  O  I
I  N  D  I  C  T  M  E  N  T  R
D  I  C  T  A  T  O  R  D  I  C
```

_____ a. act of speaking so that another may write down

_____ b. public words issued by an official and proclaiming a law or command

_____ c. to speak about future events, foretell

_____ d. to speak against; to deny the truth; to say the opposite

_____ e. a leader who speaks and rules with total power

_____ f. one's manner of speaking; enunciation

_____ g. the decision in a trial given by a jury

_____ h. a reference book in which spoken and written words are defined

_____ i. a judge's ruling or statement

_____ j. formal words spoken or written by a grand jury charging a person with a crime

dict

speak

Said the Spider to the Fly

"Will you walk into my parlor?" said the spider to the fly;
"'Tis the prettiest little parlor that ever you did spy."
So begins a famous poem of childhood. Match each comment below to the correct speaker.

a. said the ruler in the Kingdom of Kat.
b. said the suspect to the grand jury.
c. said the crystal-ball manufacturer.
d. said a scientist to his friend, Dr. Einstein.
e. said the lingerie-d lawyer.
f. said the diction coach to the beauty contestant.
g. said a little boy looking at vulgar graffiti.
h. said the ice cream shop clerk.
i. said the dictator-waiter.
j. said the boss to her secretary.

_____ 1. "Speak more clearly, dearie."

_____ 2. "Predict the future? — I don't think so. These are just plain old glass."

_____ 3. "What's the verdict? Chocolate or vanilla?"

_____ 4. "No more shorthand, Ms. Jones! I have finally purchased a dictation machine."

_____ 5. "Gee whiz, Bert. My findings contradict yours."

_____ 6. "Are these words in my school dictionary?"

_____ 7. "By royal edict, no dogs allowed!"

_____ 8. "I forbid you to order that dish! I insist you try the fish instead!"

_____ 9. "Issue an indictment or set me free."

_____ 10. "Judgie-pooh, what is your dictum on my outfit? Would pink look better?"

Legal Eagles

Fill in the blanks in the sentences below with vocabulary words and learn some legal history on the side!

1. According to ancient Babylonian law, a man who _____ the king had his tongue cut out.

2. According to the Bible, God _____ the Ten Commandments to Moses on top of Mount Sinai.

3. Moses' writings _____ that children who honored their parents would live long lives.

4. In 399 B.C., an Athenian court _____ the great philosopher Socrates for false teaching.

5. Although Socrates knew he was innocent of the charge, he accepted the _____ and submitted to the death penalty to show his respect for the law.

6. Norman conquerors of England outlawed the old Saxon _____, bringing new words and new pronunciations to the language.

7. In 1857, the U.S. Supreme Court handed down the _____ that no black person could claim U.S. citizenship.

8. Abraham Lincoln countered by issuing an _____ of his own in 1863, the Emancipation Proclamation, which paved the way for the Fourteenth Amendment to the Constitution.

9. Adolf Hitler, like most _____ throughout history, suspended laws that protected the rights of his own people.

10. Today's laws are often written with such difficult terms that lawyers themselves consult legal _____ to properly understand the rulings.

Carry On!

Since the dawn of time, the human race has been busy carrying objects from one place to another. One of the earliest words for this activity was *port*. That one root, combined with assorted prefixes and suffixes, yields many modern English words that include the idea of "carrying" in their meanings.

Use word parts from the pile of suitcases to complete the vocabulary words below. Check your answers with a dictionary.

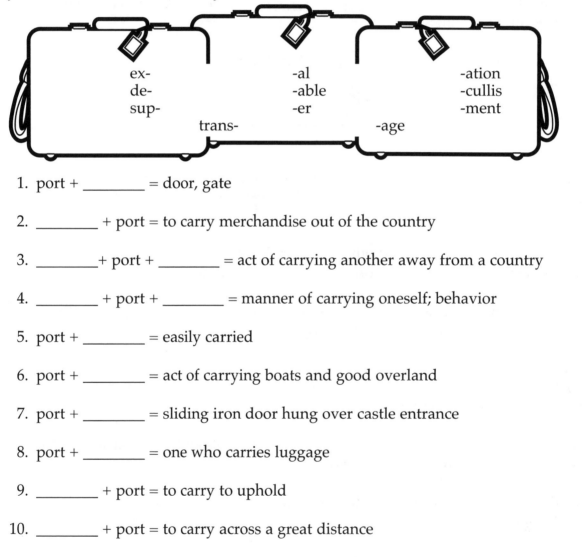

ex-
de-
sup-
trans-

-al
-able
-er

-ation
-cullis
-ment

-age

1. port + _____ = door, gate

2. _____ + port = to carry merchandise out of the country

3. _____ + port + _____ = act of carrying another away from a country

4. _____ + port + _____ = manner of carrying oneself; behavior

5. port + _____ = easily carried

6. port + _____ = act of carrying boats and good overland

7. port + _____ = sliding iron door hung over castle entrance

8. port + _____ = one who carries luggage

9. _____ + port = to carry to uphold

10. _____ + port = to carry across a great distance

Now put your new words to work. Use all ten of them in an original story. Use this sentence to get started:

> "Gee, I thought this was portable," Josh grunted to himself as he tugged and pulled on the. . . .

Sleeping Beauty

port
carry

Don't let this familiar tale fool you! There are mistakes lurking around every corner. Find and circle them. Then wave your magic wand and create a new sentence for each misused word. See if you can use those words correctly and continue the story of the sleeping princess.

1. What a wonderful evening! Everyone had brought magnificent exports to celebrate the birth of the King's new daughter.

2. But suddenly, a chilling wind whipped through a portal in the King's Grand Chamber.

3. It was Maldora, a fairy known throughout the land for her wicked deportation.

4. "Why was I not invited to this christening?" she demanded as she leaned over the portable crib of the little princess.

5. Even though Maldora was threatened with portage, she pronounced a terrible curse upon the tiny infant.

6. Years later, sewing on a tapestry of silk one day, the princess transported her finger and fell down in a deep sleep.

7. Her servants rushed to support her, but they too were suddenly overcome by sleep.

8. For one hundred years, portcullis over the entire castle until it completely hidden from view.

9. Then one day a young porter stumbled upon it as he leading his men through the woods.

10. He hacked and cleared the vines away at last, the castle deportment emerged the leaves.

port carry

Basket of Goodies

You are a reporter on the trail of a fast-breaking news story. Use the questions below to interview the eye witnesses. Write their answers in the spaces provided.

Questions for Little Red:

1. What kind of portable goodies were you taking to Granny Red? _____
   _____

2. How did you transport the goodies to Granny's house? _____
   _____

Questions for Granny Red:

3. What did you think when you heard the knocking on your portcullis? _____
   _____

4. How did it feel to come so close to heaven's portals? _____
   _____
   _____

Questions for Kind Woodsman:

5. News 6 has learned that you and your men were in the middle of a portage when you heard screams from Granny Red's house. Tell us more. _____
   _____
   _____

Questions for Woolly Wolf:

6. How do you feel about the deportation order issued against you by the State Department? _____
   _____

7. We have heard rumors that you plan to start an import/export company in your new country. Can you give us any details? _____
   _____
   _____

Questions for Mrs. Red:

8. Have you used your daughter as a porter often in the past? _____
9. Can you comment on your daughter's deportment throughout today's terrifying events? _____
   _____

10. Mrs. Red, do you support tougher wolf-control laws? _____
    _____

All Together Now

There is nothing more beautiful than assorted voices coming together in a symphony of song! The root *sym*, also spelled *syn*, gives us many modern words that share this idea of "togetherness," "sameness." Beside each definition below, write the letter of the matching vocabulary word. Check your answers with a dictionary.

a. sympathy
b. synagogue
c. syndicate
d. synthetic
e. symbiosis

f. symmetry
g. symptom
h. symposium
i. synonym
j. photosynthesis

_____ 1. a body of business people working together.
_____ 2. the coming together of light and chemicals within a plant to produce green growth.
_____ 3. the act of feeling the same emotions as another.
_____ 4. a word having the same meaning as another word.
_____ 5. a gathering together for the purpose of discussing a particular topic.
_____ 6. a condition indicating a particular disease.
_____ 7. a place where Jewish worshippers meet together.
_____ 8. having the same shape on both sides of a dividing line.
_____ 9. formed together from artificial parts, not genuine.
_____ 10. the living together in close association of two different organisms.

SYM-ART: Now for some fun! Fold a sheet of paper in half. Turn it so the fold is next to your body. Write your name on the fold. Cut along the outline of your name. DO NOT CUT THE FOLD! Open your symmetrical cut-out and mount it on colored paper. Decide what your name looks like and add details. Then write in your new words. Use your Sym-Art to help you build a better vocabulary.

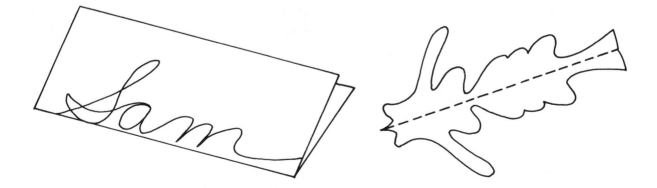

A Job Well Done

When we all pull together, it is amazing what we can accomplish! For each want ad below, fill in the missing vocabulary word.

1. Help Wanted: Four-legged lawn mowers to maintain large fields. Must be able to eat all products of _____.

2. Roommate Wanted: Night owl looking for early bird to share _____ relationship and very small apartment.

3. Hostess Position available with new restaurant opening, Tea and _____. Applicant must be handy with tea bags, hot water, and hankies. Having a good shoulder to cry on also a plus for mournful customers needing a little extra TLC.

4. Thesaurus-writer needs skilled assistant for_____-sifting. Job involves putting together long lists of words with similar meanings at the drop of a hat, with a moment's notice, in a flash or a jiff.

5. Health-care provider needed in small town plagued with assorted _____ ranging from unusual dimples to puzzling pimples.

6. Sinister soft drink _____ looking to hire perky press agent to improve its evil image. Job includes planning media events for all three companies within the group: Choke-a-Cola, Fright, and Seven-Down.

7. National sales manager needed for the amazing new _____ thread, Emphatic, completely compatible with today's tough textiles. Never tangles like cotton, never breaks like silk, never wears out like wool.

8. No rubbish! Firm has urgent need to identify and hire keynote speaker for Trash Disposium _____. Right person for the job will be a real stinker, able to hold the attention of 1,000 gathered garbagemen.

9. Pedagogue needed immediately for Decalogue classes at local _____. Applicants must pledge to refrain from lying, stealing, and coveting.

10. Weight-loss and body-shaping studio looking for fitness coach certified in Slimmetry and _____ to help clients build beautiful bodies on both left and right sides.

These rhyming riddles will produce a symphony of laughter. Write the letter of the matching pair by each definition.

_____	11. a harmless symptom	a.	a synthetic medic
_____	12. edible photosynthesis	b.	slim synonyms
_____	13. a robot doctor	c.	green cuisine
_____	14. thin, skinny, lean words	d.	a benign sign

UFO Scrapbook

No one will believe that you had an encounter with a real space alien, up close and personal. Luckily, you had your camera with you. Divide a sheet of paper into nine squares and read the descriptions below. For each one, draw the snapshot you took.

1. You were out jogging one day when a strange airship landed near a local synagogue, disrupting Friday evening services.

2. The vessel bustled with activity, as a syndicate of space creatures harvested gases from the atmosphere.

3. All the creatures were clothed in an unusual synthetic material that pulsed with neon colors.

4. One of the creatures approached you. His body parts were symmetrical, but he had more of them than humans do. Synonyms that describe his body shape are: frail, emaciated, gossamer, and scrawny.

5. The face showed symptoms of a long, rough space journey.

6. His skin color indicated that photosynthesis occurred within his body.

7. He looked down with true sympathy at a cut you had on your hand.

8. He took you on board his ship to attend some sort of symposium with other life forms from across the galaxy.

9. You listened—amazed that you could understand his strange language—as the alien lectured on how all inhabitants of the galaxy live in symbiosis.

Cupid's Arrows

Send these *phil* words shooting into your next conversation and everyone will fall in "love" with you! For each heart definition below, write the correct vocabulary word on the arrow. Check your answers with a dictionary.

a. philanthropist
b. bibliophile
c. philatelist
d. philodendron
e. philter

f. philosophy
g. philharmonic
h. philoprogenitive
i. philander

loving music

1. ⟶

lover of stamps

2. ⟶

love of wisdom

3. ⟶

to flirt, to love lightly

4. ⟶

lover of books

5. ⟶

loving one's children

6. ⟶

lover of mankind

7. ⟶

a love charm

8. ⟶

a wood-loving plant

9. ⟶

Even Cupid has to practice! On the back of your paper, use each vocabulary word in an original sentence of seven words or more.

Where Is Love?

phil
love

Use *phil* vocabulary words to fill in the blanks in the story below.

There once lived a little boy who went looking for love. His first stop was at a (1)_____'s classroom. "Can you tell me what love is?" the boy asked.

"Oh, I can tell you all about the love of wisdom," the (1)_____ said. "Is that what you are looking for?"

"No," the little boy sighed and walked on. He soon met a (2)_____, a (3)_____, and a (4)_____ conductor coming down the road. "Excuse me, gentlemen," he asked. "Do you know anything about love?"

"Love is a rare and valuable stamp," the (2)_____ said.

"No, love is lots and lots of books!" retorted the (3)_____.

"Why, it's music — pure, sweet music!" exclaimed the (4)_____ conductor.

The three men began to argue, so the little boy walked on. Soon he came to a phone booth where a (5)_____ was busy dialing numbers.

"What is love?" the little boy asked.

The (5)_____ grinned and flipped the pages of his little black book. "See the ladies' names in here? I'm dying to love them all!"

A (6)_____ overheard the conversation. "Dying—who's dying? I love people the most when they are dead! That way, they don't cause any problems."

A (7)_____ dashed up. "Problems? Are those names of people with problems? Love is giving people money to help solve problems."

But the little boy was not satisfied with any of these answers. He was looking for a special love, love that would make him feel warm and cozy and happy. He saw a leafy green (8)_____ twined tightly around a tree. Where could he find a love like that? he wondered. A sign in a store window caught his eye. "On Sale Today, Love Potions and (9)_____." The boy walked on. He was smart enough to know love could not be bought or sold.

Tired and discouraged, the little boy headed home. His mother ran to meet him, "Oh, son, I have missed you so much!"

Safe in his mother's arms, the little boy realized he had always had the best love of all, the love of a (10)_____ parent!

phil
love

History/Mysteries

Use your expertise in vocabulary to solve the history/mysteries below. You may use any reference materials you wish to locate answers.

1. What bibliophile's collection began the Library of Congress? _____

_____

2. Why do philodendrons make excellent houseplants? _____

_____

3. In what did James Smithson's philanthropy result?_____

_____

4. Briefly summarize the philosophies of the three greatest thinkers of the ancient world, Socrates, Plato, and Aristotle. _____

_____

_____

5. Which American president was a philatelist? _____

6. Why is modern China not considered a philoprogenitive country? _____

_____

7. Name two Austrian symphony composers whose work is performed by philharmonic groups all over the world._____

8. Why could King Solomon be considered one of history's greatest philanderers?

_____

_____

9. Which wife of Henry the Eighth was first accused of trapping the king with a philter and then beheaded for unfaithfulness?_____

Now write three history/mysteries of your own, using *phil* vocabulary words. Exchange papers with a classmate and try to answer each other's questions.

Answer Key

Leaf Lovers   Page 1
1. c   6. g
2. f   7. d
3. b   8. e
4. i   9. j
5. a   10. h

Comic Re-Leaf   Page 2
1. defoliant   6. unifoliate
2. trefoil   7. folio
3. foliage   8. folic acid
4. foil   9. exfoliate
5. portfolio   10. bifoliate

Turn Over a New Leaf   Page 3
2. Vitamin in leafy greens aids dancing in cold folks from Finland.
3. Tree trimmers will have plenty of business this spring due to the excellent leaf-growing season.
4. The puzzling path of red, white, and blue clovers led to a cave in the woods where three troll brothers lived.
5. Scientists who study plants do not know what to make of a rare two-leafed flower blooming in City Park.
6. Blowing away years of dust, the college janitor uncovered the notebook and pen used by the inventor of Frankenstein.
7. The town's Halloween candy has been found in an artist's briefcase out in the middle of Farmer Brown's field.
8. People against chemical leaf sprays argue to protect the wild fig trees found in area forests.
9. A football made of kitchen wrap makes it into *The Guinness Book of World Records*.
10. Lawndale Elementary cancels its autumn carnival because the cold weather has turned the area's leaves brown.

Mission to Mars   Page 4
1. f   6. e
2. h   7. i
3. d   8. b
4. j   9. a
5. c   10. g

Interplanetary P. O.   Page 5
1. permit   6. remittance
2. missiles   7. admissible
3. missives   8. submissive
4. smite   9. transmit
5. missionaries   10. Commissioner

What on Earth?   Page 6
1. g   6. i
2. d   7. b
3. e   8. f
4. a   9. j
5. h   10. c

A. She is angry that the county is raising property taxes.
B. The evidence, a chocolate cake, was accidentally eaten by the deputy.
C. Their planet is already overpopulated.
D. The missionary used the wrong ZIP code.
E. He is afraid of having his tax returns audited.

Hand in Hand   Page 7
1. f   6. c
2. j   7. a
3. g   8. e
4. b   9. h
5. i   10. d

Hand Done   Page 8
Students will add color to fingernails, draw in a handcuff and a ring, show the butterfly leaving and an ant crawling around the thumb. They add blister and wrinkle marks, the rough draft of a book with a how-to title related to business. Description: Mandy likes metal jewelry; she is kind to small creatures, a hard worker with initiative who has been given the responsibility of supervising others.

All Hands on Deck   Page 9
1. a beauty queen, so her hands will look good
2. a criminal, so he cannot reach a gun
3. a president, so he knows what bills to pass
4. a publisher, so he can print the next big best seller
5. an unhandy handyman, so he can learn from his mistakes
6. an inventor, so she can get rich from her latest invention
7. a rowdy ball team, so they will learn to behave and concentrate on the game
8. a troop of green soldiers, so they can learn proper military procedures
9. a trapped animal, so it can go free
10. a puppet, so it can move.

Write and Wrong   Page 10
1. g (1)   6. c (3)
2. j (3)   7. h (1)
3. a (2)   8. f (2)
4. e (1)   9. b (3)
5. i (2)   10. d (1)

Rest in Peace   Page 11
1. malodorous   6. malediction
2. malaria   7. malevolence
3. malapropism   8. malignant
4. malefactor   9. malady
5. malpractice   10. malicious

Pardon Me?   Page 12
1. expertise/malpractice
2. fragrant/malodorous
3. well-being/maladies
4. benedictions/maledictions
5. benign/malignant
6. good air/malaria

7. correct words/malapropisms
8. kindly/malicious
9. benefactor/malefactor
10. Benevolence/Malevolence

A. The Old Woman Who Lived in a Shoe
B. Tom the Piper's Son
C. the cook in Sing a Song of Sixpence
D. the spider in Little Miss Muffet

Birthday Blow-Out   Page 13
1. d   6. f
2. g   7. b
3. a   8. c
4. j   9. e
5. i   10. h

Star-Studded Birthday   Page 14
1. indigenous   6. generous
2. generations   7. gender
3. genius   8. genteel
4. genuine   9. progeny
5. generic   10. genesis

a. natives of Hollywood
b. GiGi likes only real things—no imitation diamonds or gold, no copies of designer labels
c. males and females; their children
d. with good manners, to impress the opposite sex
e. 75 years, a generation is usually figured as 25 years
f. 90 years old, based on the date for the Model T, 1908.

Kissing Cousins   Page 15
1. To courthouse records of births and deaths, family Bibles, cemeteries.
2. A Gentile does not celebrate Hanukkah; only Jews do.
3. He mates two winners, hoping they will pass their best traits on to their offspring.
4. Hitler; yes: Kuwait, Iraq, parts of Africa and the former Yugoslavia.
5. Students list names of their own ancestors.
6. Land and manor houses.
7. The rise of the middle class left the great estates without workers to support them.
8. An electrical generator actually does not create electricity; it simply transforms energy from mechanical to electrical.
9. Good genes for jeans might be slim hips, small waist, long legs.
10. The Old Woman Who Lived in a Shoe.

Around the World   Page 16

Across: 10, 3, 9, 5, 8
Down: 4, 7, 1, 2, 6

Where in the World?   Page 18
1. Uruguay
2. He published important books on minerals, fossils, and mining during the Renaissance.
3. To establish land boundaries after the annual flooding of the Nile and to build pyramids
4. Pierce County, North Dakota; a pile of stones marks the spot.
5. Nicolaus Copernicus.
6. Carlsbad Caverns.
7. ancient Babylon.
8. Arlington National Cemetery, Virginia.
9. Italy, Greece, Spain, France, Egypt, Libya, Algeria.
10. extremely mountainous due to the Alps.

Fancy Footwork   Page 19
1. g   6. h
2. c   7. d
3. j   8. b
4. a   9. e
5. f   10. i

Feet First   Page 20
1. podiatrist   6. pedal
2. pedestal   7. pedometer
3. pedestrian   8. impediment
4. quadruped   9. tripod
5. centipede   10. pedicure

A Foot in the Door   Page 21
1. pedals   6. tripods
2. podiatrist   7. pedestals
3. quadrupeds   8. pedometer
4. impediments   9. pedicures
5. centipedes   10. pedestrians

11. e
12. c
13. f
14. a
15. b
16. d

Stars and Stripes Forever   Page 22
a. aster   f. disaster
b. constellation   g. stelliform
c. stellar   h. asteroid
d. astronomy   i. asterisk
e. astrodome   j. astrologer

Twinkle, Twinkle   Page 23
1. astrodome   6. disaster
2. constellation   7. asteroids
3. asterisk   8. stellar
4. asters   9. astrologer
5. astronomy   10. stelliform

Now Playing: *Starstomp*   Page 24
Students' answers will vary.

Clock Wise

1. h		6. j	
2. e		7. b	
3. a		8. i	
4. g		9. c	
5. d		10. f	

Beat the Clock

anachronisms: watches, cellular phone, 0800, Einstein, Washington, Moses, psychiatrist, CD players, aspirin, radar, tape recorder

Time Out

2. The written record of a person who endlessly complains
3. A book for collectors of valuable clocks
4. Instructions for parents on how to keep children's fits of temper brief
5. A look at the armed tanks used today by the nations of the world
6. How to make beautiful music together with drinking straws
7. Learn to be a pro at making off-the-cuff speeches
8. The rhythm and speed of life in a Florida city
9. A sailor's account of memorable storms at sea
   A.*Chronic Tempest Tantrums*
   B.*Excellent Extemporaneous Exits*
   C.*Chronicles of a Chronometer Kook*

Wet and Wonderful!

1. h		6. c	
2. e		7. j	
3. a		8. b	
4. f		9. g	
5. i		10. d	

Tanks a Lot!

Students color the water blue; they draw seals, fish with rabies, a painter octopus, a water channel and a water wheel, farmer fish, a fire hydrant, stars overhead, and a lemonade stand.

The Clock Is . . . Dripping

1. hydraulic
2. aqueduct
3. hydrophobic
4. aquarelles
5. hydrant
6. hydroponic
7. Aquarius
8. aquamarine
9. aqueous
10. aquatic
11. growing plants in water
12. rabies, water supply, water color paintings
13. long-winded
14. from the stars

Power Under the Hood

1. promote		6. remote	
2. commotion		7. locomotion	
3. demote		8. automobile	
4. emotion		9. unmotivated	
5. immobile		10. nonmotile	

Motion City

1. Rocky's Rock Music Club
2. County Jail
3. School
4. School
5. Dr. Finkle's
6. Boondock's
7. Junk Yard
8. Animal & Insect Hospital
9. Train Station

Motion Sickness

1. G		6. C	
2. I		7. A	
3. E		8. F	
4. B		9. D	
5. H			

Head Hunters

1. h		6. c	
2. e		7. f	
3. g		8. j	
4. a		9. b	
5. d		10. i	

Upper Case Code

1. The capital of New Jersey is Trenton.
2. Could Superman fly without his cape?
3. "Never capitulate!" shouted General Custer.
4. Shuttle to NASA: Recapitulate safety rules ASAP!
5. Captain Charles Lindbergh made his famous flight in 1927.
6. "Lemonade for sale," called the junior capitalist.
7. The Queen of Hearts wanted to decapitate Alice.
8. Removing one's cap shows respect.
9. Fickle is a synonym for capricious.
10. What's a parade without caparisoned horses?

History/Mysteries

1. the battle of the Alamo
2. Knights of the Round Table
3. guillotine
4. Cape Horn
5. Magna Carta
6. capitalism
7. Captain John Smith
8. Civil War
9. Henry VIII
10. Philadelphia

His and Hers

1. f		6. h	
2. i		7. g	
3. b		8. a	
4. c		9. d	
5. e			

Family Matters

1. A bossy man of high birth found himself unable to move after eating a sausage biscuit at a restaurant.
2. Packages of pickles sent by pickle-lovers have piled into the Vatican.
3. Old Mr. Quark alerted police yesterday to a thief trying to steal a dog from a child playing in the park.

4. The otter acquired by our city zoo was trained by experts in Pittsburgh.
5. Nine months of pregnancy don't have to drag.
6. County officials have determined that all marriages performed last year were illegal.
7. A young mother honors her family tradition by naming her newborn triplets after their father.
8. Five months pregnant, the mayor of Littleton has announced her resignation.
9. A new product idea has hit the market with a splash. Now kids can copy art right off their underwear.

All in the Family   **Page 39**
1. A matron is a housekeeper or a prison warden. Having motherly looks would have no bearing on her job.
2. I don't want to marry now, so I'll take an inheritance from my father.
3. My grandmother; she is bossy, she has good opinions, and she loves us all.
4. I have entered Lawndale Middle School.
5. Being a father does not guarantee good fatherly instincts.
6. I shop frequently at my favorite store. I treat my brother in a condescending fashion.
7. Jessica; my mother's name is Jessie.
8. "Land where my fathers died."
9. No; not everyone who enters a school finishes and graduates.

Goody Goody Gumdrops   **Page 40**
1. f   6. d
2. c   7. j
3. a   8. h
4. i   9. e
5. b   10. g

Bon Voyage   **Page 41**
1. bona fide
2. beneficiary
3. benediction
4. bounteous
5. bonanza
6. *bon vivants*
7. benevolent
8. benign
9. benefactor
10. bonus

For Goodness' Sake   **Page 42**
1. Santa
2. Thanksgiving
3. St. Valentine
4. Columbus
5. Easter Bunny
6. Halloween trick-or-treaters
7. Martin Luther King, Jr.
8. leprechauns
9. Presidents' Day
10. February 29 on Leap Year

Play Ball!   **Page 43**
1. injection
2. eject
3. jettison
4. subject
5. dejection
6. trajectory
7. reject
8. projection
9. interjection
10. projectile

Wow! Rats! Yike!   **Page 44**
1. injection
2. jettison
3. interjections
4. projection
5. subjects
6. trajectory
7. reject
8. projectile
9. eject
10. dejection

Flotsam and Jetsam   **Page 45**
1. rejected
2. projectile
3. ejected
4. trajectory
5. injections
6. Jettison
7. projections
8. interjections
9. dejected
10. subjects, subject

Marshmallows, Please   **Page 46**
1. c   6. j
2. f   7. g
3. i   8. a
4. h   9. d
5. b   10. e

International House of Heartburn   **Page 47**
1. flammable
2. inflammations
3. Inflammatory
4. Pyrite
5. pyrophobes
6. pyrotechnics
7. flamboyant
8. Pyre
9. pyromaniac
10. pyrography

Snap, Crackle, Pop!   **Page 48**
Correct sentences: 1, 2, 4, 7, 8, 9

Blue Ribbon Specials   **Page 49**
1. g   6. e
2. c   7. j
3. h   8. f
4. d   9. i
5. a   10. b

The Princess and the Pea — Page 50

son of the king—prince; rules about government ceremonies—protocol; first, most basic—primary; first ancestors—primogenitors; very first—primeval; territories belonging to kings' sons—principalities; basic beliefs—principles; first reading book—primer; main character—protagonist; pampered, prissy woman—prima donna

First Impressions — Page 51
1. Tell her she is beautiful, buy her flowers, wait on her hand and foot.
2. Yes, fossils of ape creatures have been found believed to be 14 million years old.
3. When he is learning to read.
4. Be fair, listen to all sides,. . .
5. They cannot be reduced to more basic elements.
6. Prince Ranier.
7. Because their hip bones are very similar.
8. Answers will vary.
9. A twenty-first-century reading book will most likely be on computer.
10. The states hold first elections to narrow the field of candidates running for president.

Making Tracks — Page 52
1. e
2. j
3. f
4. h
5. g
6. a
7. b
8. c
9. i
10. d

Wheel of Fortune — Page 53
1. I will study the book of words.
2. I will call in a ghostbuster to visit the haunted tomb.
3. I will enjoy the many petals of the large flower.
4. I will eat many meals from the round tuna.
5. I will listen to everything the talkative parrot has to say.
6. I will donate the old-fashioned turning grill to a museum.
7. I will cheer any country that can make a total change without using weapons.
8. I will feel rich standing in a round room of roses.
9. I will stay away from a volcano that is beginning to develop. It's too dangerous!
10. I will use my turning rooster to wake up all my neighbors.

In the Pit — Page 54
1. e
2. h
3. i
4. b
5. f
6. a
7. c
8. g
9. d
10. j

Heartbroken — Page 55
1. e
2. h
3. c
4. j
5. f
6. a
7. b
8. g
9. i
10. d

Love Letters — Page 56
1. accordion
2. encourage
3. courage
4. concord
5. accord
6. concordance
7. record
8. discord
9. cordial
10. discouraging

By Heart — Page 57
1. Cyrillys Damian, concertina
2. the Bible
3. It resulted from the two countries agreeing to work together.
4. the Civil War
5. They think it lacks harmony.
6. Thomas Edison, 1877
7. Alfred B. Nobel
8. Emily Post, Miss Manners
9. the Bible, a biography of George Washington, *Pilgrim's Progress*, *Aesop's Fables*
10. her family, cultured young ladies of the mid-1800s lowered themselves to do such dirty work

Tyrannosaurus Rex — Page 58

Across: 2, 7, 8, 9
Down: 1, 2, 3, 4, 5, 6

Nestor, Court Jester — Page 59
1. g
2. e
3. i
4. a
5. h
6. c
7. j
8. f
9. d
10. b

Sample plot: Men in chess regalia would hide weapons under their clothes and sneak into the palace. When the king came in from exercising the regal eagle, the men would jump out and. . . .

King for a Day — Page 60
Samples (actual answers will vary):
1. strait-jackets
2. 8 hours of exercise a day
3. give them one million dollars apiece
4. ban all weapons
5. kids could drive at age 12
6. every citizen would be required to have dog biscuits available at all times
7. rudeness, tardiness
8. when the king rode by
9. I would outlaw all round shapes—everything would be made with four corners
10. Party hearty!

One-Track Mind — Page 61

1. c
2. e
3. g
4. j
5. h
6. a
7. i
8. d
9. b
10. f

As the Stomach Churns — Page 62

1. monocle
2. monogamy
3. monastery
4. unique
5. monopoly
6. monolith
7. union
8. monotone
9. unison
10. monophobe

One of a Kind? — Page 63

1. uniform/j
2. monarch/d
3. monosyllabic/f
4. universe/e
5. monomania/g
6. monogram/i
7. unicorn/c
8. monotheism/a
9. monologue/b
10. monochromatic/h

Twice as Nice — Page 64

1. f
2. j
3. i
4. a
5. h
6. c
7. g
8. d
9. e
10. b

Double Trouble — Page 65

1. e, she leads music for two singers
2. b, he wants to end trickery
3. h, he/she is carrying a baby in the car
4. j, she stops for people who speak two languages
5. d, he enjoys fighting one opponent
6. a, the dentist has worked on her tooth
7. f, he enjoys the exchange of ideas between two people
8. i, she is advertising the town's big birthday
9. c, an old country boy likes his new glasses
10. g, a weight lifter enjoys building his arm muscles

Show and Tell — Page 66

Samples (actual answers will vary):

1. a two-legged creature with glasses: "Oh, there they are! I can finally see my feet!"
2. two people: "Parlez-vous Français?" "No."
3. a dentist pulling out a stubborn tooth: "This won't hurt a bit!"
4. a cake with 200 candles: "Where's the fire extinguisher?"
5. two cats howling: "Get a pet rabbit instead!"
6. one boy with a girl on each arm: "What a two-timing snake!"
7. a baby with large muscles: "These bodybuilders get younger every day!"

Paint By Number — Page 67

1. e/red
2. d/yellow
3. j/blue
4. g/blue
5. f/orange
6. i/green
7. c/red
8. a/green
9. b/orange
10. h/yellow

The Scoop Shoppe — Page 68

1. f
2. j
3. e
4. a
5. b
6. h
7. i
8. c
9. g
10. d

244 flavors

Your Lucky Number — Page 69

1. 3
2. 100
3. 5
4. 10
5. 100
6. 3
7. 4
8. 5
9. 10
10. 4
11. 10
12. 3
13. 100
14. 10
15. 5

Through the Looking Glass — Page 70

1. g
2. d
3. e
4. h
5. j
6. b
7. a
8. f
9. i
10. c

A Closer Look — Page 71

1. spectators
2. conspicuous
3. suspicious
4. spectacle
5. specter
6. retrospective
7. spectrum
8. specimen
9. speculate
10. speculum

The Specter Inspector — Page 72

1. b
2. f
3. a
4. c
5. d
6. e

Top Secret — Page 73

1. e
2. i
3. c
4. b
5. g
6. j
7. d
8. h
9. a
10. f

Last Will and Testament — Page 74

1. autographed
2. autobiography
3. cardiograms
4. graphology
5. epigraph
6. grammar
7. paragraphs
8. graphics
9. orthography
10. biographies

With Pen in Hand — Page 75

1. d
2. g
3. b
4. h
5. f
6. a
7. i
8. c
9. j
10. e

Mr. Tee — Page 76

1. d
2. f
3. b
4. h
5. e
6. a
7. i
8. g
9. c

Meet Me at the Mall   Page 77
1. b   6. a
2. h   7. f
3. d   8. c
4. i   9. g
5. e

Simon Says   Page 78
Students follow pantomime directions.

In the Running   Page 79
1. c   6. d
2. e   7. j
3. h   8. f
4. a   9. i
5. g   10. b

Rhymes on the Run   Page 80
1. Lone Ranger
2. Paul Revere
3. Sacagawea
4. Mr. Ed
5. Benedict Arnold
6. Emmett Kelly
7. Tom Sawyer, Huckleberry Finn
8. Alice
9. Mickey Mouse
10. Blackbeard

Mixed Messages   Page 81
Incorrect-1, 2, 4, 6, 7, 8, 10

The Golden Rule   Page 82
1. i   6. c
2. b   7. h
3. d   8. a
4. g   9. j
5. e   10. f

On Cloud Nine   Page 83
1. archrival   6. hierarchy
2. archangel   7. archives
3. archipelago   8. archenemy
4. monarch   9. anarchy
5. Architect   10. archetype

History/Mysteries   Page 84
1. Queen Liliuokalani
2. Mayan & Lefoten
3. Tradition has it that an unknown architect designed the
   tomb for Shah Jahan's favorite wife.
4. the Declaration of Independence and the Constitution
5. Michael and Gabriel
6. Bluto
7. William McKinley
8. Henry Ford's Model T
9. the Montagues and the Capulets
10. baron, viscount, earl, marquis, duke

By the Book   Page 85
1. e   6. d
2. i   7. j
3. b   8. c
4. g   9. h
5. a   10. f

The Hall of the Horrid   Page 86
1. i   6. b
2. g   7. e
3. c   8. h
4. f   9. a
5. d   10. j

Twister   Page 87
Students' drawings will vary.

Small Change   Page 88
1. e   6. h
2. i   7. f
3. d   8. j
4. a   9. b
5. c   10. g

It's a Small World   Page 89
1. minor   6. minuscule
2. minister   7. minimum
3. minute   8. miniature
4. minus   9. minstrels
5. minced   10. minuet

a. 4   f. 3
b. 5   g. 10
c. 2   h. 9
d. 6   i. 8
e. 1   j. 7

Fore!   Page 90
Students play game.

Do You Hear What I Hear?   Page 91
1. c   6. i
2. e   7. a
3. h   8. j
4. b   9. d
5. f   10. g

Sounds Phishy to Me!   Page 92
1. aphonia   6. symphony
2. euphony   7. cacophony
3. xylophone   8. homophone
4. phonolite   9. phonics
5. antiphony   10. microphone

Telephony Baloney   Page 93
1. microphone   6. symphony
2. homophone   7. euphony
3. xylophone   8. cacophony
4. phonolite   9. phonics
5. aphonia   10. antiphonal

Human Beans   Page 94
1. f   6. g
2. j   7. b
3. e   8. h
4. a   9. c
5. d   10. i

A Whale of a Tale   Page 95
1. *Homo sapiens*
2. anthropologists
3. humanitarian
4. homicide
5. misanthrope
6. homage
7. anthropophagous
8. anthropomorphic
9. humane
10. anthropocentric

Human Headlines   Page 96
1. An unknown scientist of early man now feels there is no connection between man and monkey.
2. Earthlings are not the only ones to think they are the center of the universe. Scientists now report that residents of the planet Saturn feel exactly the same way.
3. As April Fool's stunt, Congressmen yesterday passed a fake bill granting the rights of citizenship to the eastern mosquito.
4. It has been discovered that Eskimo dogs do not respond well to human beings who display ill temper.
5. The police suspect that old Mr. McDonald was murdered over an improperly prepared egg dish.
6. Celebrate the goodness of country with homestyle cooking and sewing.
7. Several local doctors, known for their care and concern for teens, have petitioned the school board to eliminate all tests and homework.
8. If you cannot remember who these people are, just think of a jungle missionary bubbling away in a big black pot.
9. South Dakotans send their beloved town librarian off on her honeymoon amidst cheers and tears.

Speak Your Mind!   Page 97
1. f
2. b
3. d
4. a
5. j
6. h
7. c
8. g
9. e
10. i

Said the Spider to the Fly   Page 98
1. f
2. c
3. h
4. j
5. d
6. g
7. a
8. i
9. b
10. e

Legal Eagles   Page 99
1. contradicted
2. dictated
3. predicted
4. indicted
5. verdict
6. diction
7. dictum
8. edict
9. dictators
10. dictionaries

Carry On!   Page 100
1. portal
2. export
3. deportation
4. deportment
5. portable
6. portage
7. portcullis
8. porter
9. support
10. transport

Sleeping Beauty   Page 101
Incorrect-1, 3, 5, 6, 8, 9, 10

Basket of Goodies   Page 102
Answers will vary.

All Together Now   Page 103
1. c
2. j
3. a
4. i
5. h
6. g
7. b
8. f
9. d
10. e

A Job Well Done   Page 104
1. photosynthesis
2. symbiosis
3. Sympathy
4. synonym
5. symptoms
6. syndicate
7. synthetic
8. symposium
9. synagogue
10. symmetry

11. d
12. c
13. a
14. b

UFO Scrapbook   Page 105
Drawings will vary.

Cupid's Arrows   Page 106
1. g
2. c
3. f
4. i
5. b
6. h
7. a
8. e
9. d

Where Is Love?   Page 107
1. philosopher
2. philatelist
3. bibliophile
4. philharmonic
5. philanderer
6. philanthropist
7. philodendron
8. philters
9. philoprogenitive

History/Mysteries   Page 108
1. Thomas Jefferson's
2. They do not require intensive sunlight.
3. the Smithsonian Institute in Washington, D. C.
4. Socrates believed that abstract ideas could be pinned down by debating sharp, careful questions. Plato taught that ideas were more real and important than things. Aristotle believed that working hard brought happiness and goodness.
5. F. D. Roosevelt
6. because the government regulates the number of children a family is allowed to have
7. Haydn and Mozart
8. because he married 1,000 wives
9. Anne Boleyn